FATS WALLER

FATS
WALLER

THE CHEERFUL

LITTLE EARFUL

ALYN SHIPTON

continuum
LONDON • NEW YORK

Continuum
The Tower Building, 11 York Road, London, SE1 7NX
370 Lexington Avenue, New York, NY 10017-6503

Originally published in Britain in 1988 by Spellmount Ltd.
First paperback edition published in 1989 by Omnibus Press Ltd.
Revised edition published in 2002 by Continuum, by arrangement
with Bayou Press Ltd

British Library Cataloguing-in-Publication Data
A catalogue record for this book is available from the British Library.

ISBN 0-8264-5796-7

Library of Congress Cataloging-in-Publication Data
Shipton, Alyn
   Fats Waller/Alyn Shipton.
      p. cm. —
   Includes bibliographical references (p.) and index.
   ISBN 0-8264-5796-7
   1. Waller, Fats, 1904–1943.   2. Jazz musicians—United
States—Biography.   I. Title.   II. Series.

   ML417.W15 S5 2002
   786.2′165′092—dc21   2001047404

Typeset by BookEns Ltd, Royston, Herts
Printed and bound in the United States

CONTENTS

To Siobhan, Christopher, and Elisabeth for putting up with me while this was being written, and to my parents for introducing me to the sounds of Fats Waller at an early age

ACKNOWLEDGMENTS

Although 1986, when I started work on the original edition of this book, was late in the day to begin research on a life of Fats Waller, and many of his sidemen and intimates had passed on, it was still possible to find people who had known him. I must first of all express my gratitude to Fats's former sidemen, Harry Dial, Al Casey, and Jabbo Smith, whom I interviewed especially for this project. I am also indebted to Franz Jackson, and to Bill Coleman and Snub Mosley with whom, during various odd moments on the international jazz circuit in the late 1970s and early 1980s, I had the chance to talk about Fats and his career. I am also indebted to Sammy Price for his hospitality and his enthusiasm as the best guide to Harlem one could wish for, and to Buck Clayton, Arthur Rollini, and Danny Barker for sparing the time to talk about this book in the midst of preparing theirs.

I am particularly grateful to Mark Tucker and Garvin Bushell for sharing with me transcripts of the interviews for Garvin's autobiography (published subsequently as *Jazz from the Beginning*), and for permission to reproduce extracts from those interviews.

I am grateful to John Chilton, Max Harrison, John Holley, and Howard Rye for leading me to out-of-the-way bibliography, and for general help and support. I am equally grateful to Max Jones for his time, when not in the best of health, and to Caroline Richmond, Dave Bennett, and Frank Driggs. I also owe a debt of gratitude to Barry

Kernfeld of *The New Grove Dictionary of Jazz*, who has offered both bibliographical and discographical advice. Thanks are also due to James Lincoln Collier for his hospitality, help with research in the US press, and for some stimulating arguments. The librarians and staff of the Westminster Central Reference Library are also due my thanks.

I am grateful to the readers of the first edition who wrote to me with new and additional information, and to Laurie Wright, with whom I corresponded during the preparation of his monumental *Fats in Fact* (1992). That book has added significantly to the body of information about Waller, and I have consulted it frequently.

All the mistakes and errors of facts and judgment are mine.

The pictures in this book come principally from the Max Jones Collection, Jazz Music Books, the *Melody Maker*, the author's collection, and, in alphabetical order: Dave Bennett, Buck Clayton, Teresa Chilton, Nancy Miller Elliott, and Caroline Richmond. The illustrations are reproduced by permission. Every effort has been made to trace copyright holders and the author and publishers apologize to anyone whose name may have been inadvertently omitted from this list.

The "Harmful Little Armful."

INTRODUCTION

There have been more books devoted to the life and works of Fats Waller than almost any other figure in the history of jazz. So when I began thinking about writing the first edition of this book in 1986, I asked myself if there really was a need for another one.

Starting with Charles Fox's excellent short biography from 1960, which was followed up in 1966 by the large tome of reminiscence written mainly by Waller's one-time manager Ed Kirkeby and augmented by Duncan Schiedt, Sinclair Traill, and (with a comprehensive discography) John R. T. Davies, the ground had been well prepared for the arrival of two further volumes in 1977. The first of these was by Waller's son Maurice and Anthony Calabrese, and the second by Joel Vance.

Was there any more to be said about Waller?

What prompted me to think that there was came in the form of a short musicological survey by Paul S. Machlin, called *Stride*, which I had a hand in publishing for the UK market in 1985. That book took a detailed look at Waller's improvisatory methods, and drew attention to several aspects of his playing, not least his innovative approach to the pipe organ. By the time Machlin's survey appeared, almost all Waller's extant recordings had become available on microgroove, following the laudable attempts by the French RCA company to issue his complete commercially recorded *oeuvre*, and from an equally determined effort by some smaller independent labels to issue his broadcasts and unofficial discs. This was a body of material that had not been readily available to earlier writers, and it allowed for an assessment of Waller's musical life based on the ability to hear every stage of his recorded work in order. The time seemed, after all, to be right to look again at this giant of jazz history.

In particular, I wanted to challenge some of the assumptions made in Kirkeby's book, and carried forward into the other biographies I have mentioned, about the dating of Waller's early tours, about his mid-1920s visits to Chicago, his imprisonment in the late 1920s, his career in the musical theater, and the formation of his first big band. As it turns out, my investigations were largely corroborated when in 1992 Laurie Wright published the results of his life's interest in Waller, in the bio-discography *Fats in Fact*. That is very much a specialist work, but I have consulted it in revising my text, which, as before, is aimed at a more general reader.

All this means that, in some respects, I have concentrated less than is customary on anecdotes about the larger-than-life aspects of Waller's career, and a little more on the extraordinary professionalism and skill he brought to every aspect of his music-making. Every biographer of Waller has been impressed with his playing – he was, after all, the leading stride pianist of his generation – but he deserves equal consideration as a master songwriter, show composer, and recording and broadcasting artist.

Despite these serious aspects of Waller's legacy, his abiding gift to the generations that followed is his boisterous good humor. It is a rare talent to make an audience laugh aloud at an aside on a gramophone record. That Waller could manage this feat often, and that his irrepressible *bonhomie* has stood the test of the decades that have passed since his death, is a tribute to his rarest quality of all – the ability to communicate his enormous talent and personality to every listener. When his recordings are played today on the radio, he can still make one face the day with a smile, and his own philosophical outlook: "Well, *All* right, then!"

Fats in the early 1920s.

EARLY LIFE
IN HARLEM

S tand at the crossroads of Fifth Avenue and 135th Street in Harlem today, and you will see about you all the trappings of a fairly prosperous suburb. On one corner, the Chase Manhattan Bank; opposite, a small row of shops. On the north-eastern corner, the tall apartment blocks of 2225 Fifth Avenue rise solidly over the neighborhood. This crossroads is at the very center of Harlem, nowadays a predominantly African-American district of Manhattan, bounded on the south by Central Park, on the north by 155th Street, and stretching across from St Nicholas Avenue over to the East River.

As Harlem moves into the twenty-first century, fewer of its streets are depressed and squalid. A few blackened shells of empty buildings wait for the real-estate sharks or the redevelopers to move in, but the atmosphere is energetic, and filled with hope. The street life is full of the contrasts that make up the patchwork of New York City. Soul music, hip-hop and rap swell from open doorways, and the streets are alive with the endless twenty-four-hour bustle of all Manhattan.

You could pass by in a bus, a taxi, or an automobile, and see little evidence of Harlem's glamorous past. Where now is the glitter of the Cotton Club? The Lafayette? The Lincoln? The first largely torn down, the last two now converted to churches. The shadows of the Alhambra

Theater and the block where the doors have closed for the last time on Smalls' Paradise make it seem as if Harlem's glories, its legends, have vanished for good. Even the too-perfect shining houses of "Striver's Row" on 139th Street, the monument to the endeavors of the African-American community, seem little more than a token reminder of Harlem's history.

As with any community, the vicissitudes of time and fashion cannot completely harm it. The strength of the old Harlem was in its people – the African-American population which adopted this once prosperous northern suburb and made it its own. Go into one of the small bars or diners in the little group of shops on 135th Street, and it is there, in the soul and spirit of the people, that you will find what remains of Harlem's history.

The buildings that stand on this crossroads at the center of Harlem cover the site of Leroy's, the legendary nightspot where Willie "the Lion" Smith held sway at the piano, and where the young Fats Waller played his first cabaret job. Although the buildings have gone, the memories have not. In the mid-1980s the pianist Sammy Price lived right across the street. "Fats Waller? He had soul a plenty, technique in large proportions. Rhythm was really his business, and his singing voice was tops. He did pretty good on the organ too!"[1]

As Sammy Price guided me around the area, we met other friends of Fats. Stanley Shepherd, for instance, the younger brother of Fats's chauffeur Buster, hung out in one of the bars there. "Yeah, Fats! He used to pay us kids just to do a little sand dance on the street corners as he came home . . . he was kicks."[2] And just like the old anecdote about Waller's memorial service where sadness changed to mirth as one after another of the funny stories about his rich and varied life tumbled out, everyone in the bar gathered around Stanley and joined in with his or her memories of Waller and the old days in Harlem.

Fats Waller was an outsize man in almost all respects. Five foot eleven inches tall, he is reputed to have weighed 285 pounds at the time of his death. His *New York Times* obituary marveled at his digital dexterity, given the size of his plump fingers. He was unquestionably the greatest of the Harlem jazz pianists and had a talent as pianist and organist in direct proportion to his physical stature. In addition, Fats had an outsize personality. He was generous, funny, vulgar, and in many ways selfish, but in everything that he did he was larger than life. Stories of the kind that flowed in the 135th Street bar tell of his gargantuan appetites. He womanized, he ate vast meals, and perhaps most noticeably he drank huge quantities of alcohol. The stories may exaggerate, but one after another they tell of the gin on the piano, the bottles of scotch in the recording studio, the "liquid ham and eggs." When Fats's third son Ronald was asked at school what his father did, the boy thought there was nothing strange about his entirely truthful reply, "He drinks gin."[3]

But if Fats displayed larger-than-life appetites, and went through much of his life unruffled by a daily alcoholic intake that would have killed most normal people in a few days; if he was thoughtless in the treatment of his first wife and son while profligate in his generosity to the poor and to underprivileged children; if he was capable of shouting vulgar jokes over keyboard accompaniments that were dazzling in their virtuosity, nevertheless Fats Waller was a man loved by millions. To those who knew him and those who did not, this maverick, complicated personality, and musical genius commands fierce loyalty and affection, even today.

Like his contemporary Louis Armstrong, Fats was one of the first of the great jazzmen to break through to a wider public, and to become a popular entertainer of international stature. And just like Louis, Fats was a mass of apparent contradictions. At one level, he was a serious contemplative keyboard player and composer, whose prodigious natural gifts were enhanced by the rigorous training of classical study on the one hand and Harlem nightlife on the other. As well as being the composer of a string of popular hits, Fats was remembered as a craftsman among songwriters, perfecting each note of a written copy so that it was precise and exact for the printer. But he was also legendary for reneging on contracts, a man whom promoters wouldn't hire twice after seeing him jump into his car before the show, shouting to his

The author and Sammy Price at the junction of Fifth Avenue and 135th Street near the site of Leroy's.

chauffeur, "Buster! Holland Tunnel," and disappearing in a cloud of dust for New York. A master of the emergent art of radio broadcasting, Fats occasionally overstepped the bounds of taste or humor. Perhaps nothing underlines the contradictions more perfectly than the story that even when seated at his favorite and most serious instrument, the organ, he was frequently ticked off for disposing of empty gin bottles into the pipework.

So why has his work survived? And why has he commanded so much love and affection through the years?

Partly, the reason is an extraordinary recorded legacy. For his period, Fats was a prolific phonograph artist, and his records have seldom been unavailable since his death in 1943. For the rest, some of the reasons may be found in the story of his life and times, and his mastery of jazz, the musical theater, and the recording studio.

It was 1920 when Waller first came to Leroy's, at the suggestion of his mentor James P. Johnson. Johnson was the "dean" of the school of brilliant pianists known as the Harlem "stride" players. Most of these men had been born in the last two decades of the nineteenth century, and had served their apprenticeship as what they perceived as being ragtime players. Ragtime was a piano style that grew up in the 1880s and largely centered around the towns of the Midwest, St Louis, Indianapolis, and New Sedalia, where such luminaries as Scott Joplin, Louis Chauvin, May Aufderheide, and James Scott held sway. Picked up by the "Eastern" ragtimers, among whom was the young pianist and composer Eubie Blake, the style made its way to New York and was taken up by Johnson, the Lion, and Luckey Roberts as well as some lesser-known figures: Abba Labba, Lippy Boyette, Willie Gant, Jack the Bear, "Beetle" Henderson, Corky Williams, Bob Hawkins, Joe Turner, and Russell Brooks.

As late as 1917, James P. Johnson was making piano rolls of pure ragtime compositions, but during World War I, as the focus of African-American cabaret and club life moved uptown from the 53rd Street area known as the "Jungles" to the very center of Harlem, the stride piano style crystallized into something recognizable in its own right.

The Joint Is Jumpin': a 1941 film recreation of a rent party. Fats, gin in hand, gets up from the piano.

The oompah left hand of ragtime became more complex and varied, the patterns less regular, and the intricate right-hand parts became more difficult too. Just as the ragtime pianists of the Midwest had taken one another on at competitive "cutting contests" to determine the most virtuoso or bravura performers, so the stride players of New York developed a fierce competitive rivalry. This became adopted into the traditions of the style. Musicians had not only to play a written composition brilliantly, as the ragtimers did, note for note, but had also to be equally competent to improvise their own variations in the same style, and to do so in a manner that would outplay any possible competition. The celebrated players found great success and fortune in the cabarets of Harlem, and also at a unique institution that grew up there as a consequence of the intensity of African-American housing – the rent party.

To understand the rent party fully, it is important to realize that Harlem was originally developed as a prosperous white suburb of New York City. Its big avenues, Seventh and Lenox, were the consequence of a generous town-planning policy that encouraged wide boulevards with plenty of trees and two carriageways to be built. In the original area to be developed, at the end of the nineteenth century, spacious housing was erected, designed for people who wanted to live away from the main business areas but have easy access to them, via the elevated railroad to 129th Street.

To capitalize on the boom, the first years of the twentieth century saw widespread building, infilling the area between Harlem and downtown Manhattan, and extending northwards. Property developers and real-estate men pushed the price of land and buildings higher and higher, until around 1904 when the bottom fell out of the market. Desperate realtors, anxious to recoup their investment, turned to the African-American community to buy up the property, and the result was a fifteen-year influx of African-Americans to the area, first as owners, but later renting sections of the large new developments at a density never envisaged by the original planners. George Hoefer, the biographer of Willie "the

Lion" Smith, estimated that by 1920, 300,000 people were in housing built for 60,000.[4]

Of course, squeezed up maybe five to a room, people still managed somehow to fall behind with the rent. To make money quickly and get out of trouble, the rent party was developed. The principle was simple – a charge was made at the door of an apartment for admission to a party at which everyone had a good time. A piano, and the best pianists in the area, were provided by way of entertainment, and at the end, not only had most of the neighborhood enjoyed themselves, but also the shortfall in the rent had been made up in admission charges. As time went by, these events were sometimes promoted for their own sake as purely commercial ventures, and they provided a source of steady employment for the pianists of Harlem.

At that time, Striver's Row (139th Street between Seventh and Eighth avenues) was still full of the original strivers. As James P. Johnson put it, "[They] strived like hell to pay the rent and taxes. They were the days of bathtub gin and corn whisky and stills in the apartments. ... The parties attracted a lot of people, many white folk who were taking up the Negro."[5] It was only later, in the 1930s, that these houses took up their present appearance, described by guitarist Danny Barker as "a row of beautiful greystone houses, clean and well maintained."[6]

In the apartment set aside for the party, there would be soul food and plenty to drink. The more commercially organized events provided women as well. The pianists would work in turns to keep the entertainment going, trying to "cut" each other for good measure. "I don't believe pianists today spend as much time with their instruments as we did," said the Lion, "for we played in places all day long and half of the night. Yes, we would wake up on the piano, and then we went to bed on the piano ... talk about those rent parties – why, we even chipped in and bought the tickets!"[7]

It was in this atmosphere that Fats grew up, and when James P. Johnson brought him down the steps into Leroy's basement to hear the

Lion, it was 1920, the year of Fats's sixteenth birthday. "Jimmy Johnson brought him in," said the Lion, "and when I noticed his pants weren't pressed, I immediately named him 'Filthy.' It was love at first sight with us. Yes! That was our bunch. 'Filthy,' 'The Brute' (that was Jimmy Johnson), and 'The Lion' (yours truly)."[8]

The young Fats was persistent, despite his lack of sartorial elegance, and he went up after the Lion and played *Carolina Shout*, the fiendishly difficult test piece composed by James P. Johnson. He "made Jimmy like it, and he made me like it," remembered Smith. Fats may have been only sixteen, but the experienced players of the rent party circuit could see that here was a talent to be reckoned with. When the Lion went away for a while, Fats took his place. Lil May Johnson, the wife of James P., was working at Leroy's as a singer. Awed by his new-found responsibility, Fats was a bit daunted by taking over the gig. "Fats was afraid to perform," recalled Lil, "so I taught him to play for me. That's how he started."[9]

How was it, then, that a sixteen-year-old came to be the protégé of the two leading Harlem pianists, playing cabaret jobs at a tender age, and displaying such signs of skill?

Thomas Wright Waller had been born on May 21, 1904. His parents were Adeline Waller and the lay preacher Edward Waller. Edward had his own trucking business, but his real interest was the church. Originally members of the Abyssinian Baptist Church on West 40th Street, to which the family continued to go even after moving to Harlem, they had transferred their worship to the Refuge Temple at 56 West 133rd Street in the heart of Harlem. Edward Waller was a pillar of his church, and conducted open-air services, reputedly preaching at the corner of Lenox Avenue and 135th Street. In common with many families in Harlem at the turn of the century, the Wallers produced a large number of children. The young Thomas was the seventh of eleven children, of whom only five survived beyond infancy. This statistic is confirmed in the biography of his father by Maurice Waller; most other accounts suggest there were twelve children.[10] The family had settled at 107 West 134th Street, virtually next door to Public School 89, which Fats (as he quickly became known) attended until he was fourteen. Adeline was concerned that her offspring should not grow up among the children whose home was on the streets of Harlem, and until the birth of her last child, Edith (which severely weakened her), in 1910, she made stringent efforts to keep her children confined to the apartment, or the school next door, where they could be supervised.

The journalist Al Hoyt discovered that his mother had known the Waller family, and interviewed her about the young Fats.

> Her recollections would go back … to the brownstone where Fats's family attended Pentecostal services in the front parlor of one of the church members' homes, and where Fats played his earliest piano "dates."
>
> My mother remembers the tall, brownskin Elder Waller as a gentle and generous man, dedicated to his family and to his religious beliefs. She remembers Fats's youthful but already rotund figure and she smiled at the recaptured image of his irrepressible joviality.

Mrs. Hoyt's recollections go on to tell how the noise of the services forced the community to move to a "storefront" nearby, where they could sustain themselves and their services.[11]

Although the church filled much of the Waller family's life, they discovered early on that young Thomas had a keen interest in music, and the piano in particular. Duncan Schiedt, the photographer and co-author of Waller's biography, told in a *Record Changer* article how the Wallers' first piano arrived complete with revolving stool. The stool provided plenty of games and amusement for the young family. Fats on one occasion spun his two sisters round until the stool collapsed, imperiling the young baby Edith. Waller got out of trouble with an assumed piety that diverted his mother from punishment to prayer.

Fats played the piano at his public school, but it was not until the death of his mother in 1920 that he really began to immerse himself in the Harlem stride tradition. After a row with his father, he moved out of the family home, and into the house of the stride pianist Russell Brooks, the elder brother of a former classmate of Fats's. Thomas was just sixteen. He began to study the piano seriously, using the Brooks's pianola to stop the action in mid-tune with the keys depressed, and, by fitting his fingers to the notes, to teach himself the fingering patterns of the piano giants who had cut the rolls. Foremost among these players was James P. Johnson, the composer of *Carolina Shout*, the piece with which Fats won his first talent contest at the Roosevelt Theater.

Soon Russell Brooks introduced Fats to Johnson. The introduction was further helped by the fact that Fats had begun to be a hanger-on at the Lincoln Theater, where he played intermissions for the pianist Mazie Mullins (who accompanied the silent movies) and occasionally sat at the organ, playing between films and deputizing for the regular organist when there was one, or filling in when there was not. Lil May Johnson recalled that "right after James P. heard Fats playing the pipe organ, he came home and told me, 'I know I can teach that boy.'"[12] Slowly James P. imparted all the technique of the stride pianist. The solid left hand, the intricate patterns that the right hand performed as endless melodic variation, and the classic cutting-contest pieces. Johnson was reputed to have a "cutting" piece in every key, so that no matter how his opponents tried, James P. could always match them. Some of this prowess rubbed off on Fats, and so did many of Johnson's other values: a love of the classics, a respect for musical literacy, and (so far as the piano was concerned) a taste and delicacy of touch that allowed Fats the full dynamic range in his playing.

The young boy's talent was noticed by the discerning participants in the Harlem rent party circuit. Eubie Blake remembered,

> I've known him from the time he was a kid. I think he had on short pants. (Boys wore short pants until they were fifteen or sixteen years of age in those days.) He could play the piano very well when he was a kid. He and Jimmy Johnson (James P. I mean) used to play what were known as house rent parties. Fats

developed into a good pianist. One of the few pianists in those days who read music, without spelling it out note by note. His left hand was superior. A perfect left hand![13]

Slowly but surely the young Waller grew in physical and musical stature. And, in a sense, he developed two simultaneous careers. In one he was to become an accomplished member of the élite circle of Harlem stride pianists; in the other he was to be hailed as a fine theater organist, brilliant not only at the art of accompanying the silent movies with wit and aplomb, but also at transferring the art of jazz improvisation to the organ.

Even at this distance in time, it is possible to get some impression of what the young Waller was actually like. Apart from the Lion's views of Fats's clothing and his "filthy" appearance, we know that in the early days of his professional life in Harlem, Waller remained in the short trousers remembered by Eubie Blake. Even as a young adult, Fats retained some childish habits, such as his propensity for turning up to work with an "apple on a stick," and many of his Harlem contemporaries recalled similar weaknesses.

Others remember his ready wit, although his fondness for *risqué* jokes and patter did not endear him to everyone. He had made part of his reputation on the rent party circuit by playing a bawdy song called *The Boy in a Boat*. The lyrics were well known in Harlem: "You ought to see the boy in a boat, he doesn't wear a hat or a coat." It was always a source of private amusement that this hymn to clitoral stimulation was preserved for posterity with different lyrics as *Squeeze Me*. Even more amusing for Fats and his friends was the unwitting advertisement of the origins of the song by the QRS piano roll company, who religiously printed the subtitle *A Boy in a Boat* on the label of Fats's 1926 piano roll of *Squeeze Me* (QRS 3352).

Even as the young Fats was becoming famous on the Harlem circuit as a talented pianist and organist he was establishing himself as a Harlem character. He was familiar to many people, since he had worked between music engagements as a delivery boy for the Harlem

Delicatessen run by George and Connie Immerman (the story going that his ample frame, even as a youth, was ideal for concealing the bootleg liquor in which they specialized).

As Fats made his rounds of Harlem clubs, he became known for his line in patter – such as his greeting:

How ya doin', good to see ya.
How's your family?
How's your wife?
How's your cousin?
How's your landlord?
How's your undertaker?
You're lookin' real prosperous, but you're gettin' uglier every day!

(a memory of Fats which was recalled by the guitarist Danny Barker).[14]

Fats's acquaintance with the Immermans and their illicit supply of liquor may have had something to do with the development of his famous capacity for liquid refreshment. He may not have been drinking much at the age of sixteen when he started playing at Leroy's, but within a year or two he was well into his lifelong habit. The stories are legion:

When Fats's band bus was all full up and ready to roll, a truck marked "Ballantines" would pull up and deliver more than a few cases of whisky. (Danny Barker)[15]

Fats had written into his contract the stipulation that he must have two fifths of gin sitting on the piano before he played. (Claude Hopkins)[16]

Fats is the only man who used to buy cases of half-pints of liquor. They called them "Mickeys," and whenever Fats would uncork a half that was one drink for him; when he put that bottle to his lips it never came down until it was finished. ... If you wanted a drink, he'd hand you a fresh bottle. (Joe Darensbourg)[17]

He'd get twelve quarts of whisky a day. (Coleman Hawkins)[18]

Much later in his career, Fats strode into a New York club, ignoring, as he passed towards the bar, the British trumpeter Nat Gonella, who was on holiday in New York only shortly after one of Waller's English tours, on which the two men had jammed together. On his way *out* of the bar, Waller greeted Gonella like an old friend. When Nat asked why Fats had ignored him on the way in, Waller explained, "I never recognize anyone until I've got a few drinks under my belt."[19]

In Fats's own mind, the first professional work he had as a musician was as the organist at the Lincoln Theater. He told Hugh Conover in a 1943 radio interview:

> I was born in Harlem kicking and screaming. I quit the kicking, but I'm still screaming . . . or moaning and groaning.
>
> When I was approximately fourteen (that's a good word that approximately, I like that) I took a job playing in a theater, and that was when I first got into trouble. My father was a minister, and he had no use for theaters. He came there and took hold of me and said, "Son, you come on home out of this den of iniquity" . . . [that didn't kill my interest in the theater] . . . I kept right on playing the piano and organ and writing songs.[20]

The early performances there, such as those which Lil May Johnson suggests were her husband's first experience of his young protégé, were also recalled by the theater's then advertising manager, Harrison Smith. The films shown at the Lincoln (according to Smith) were generally of the serial type, and it could take about fifteen weeks to see a picture right through.

> Many folks had ants in their pants to see the following chapter. One always around was Tommy Waller, skipping school or his violin lesson . . . Tommy would grab a seat near Mazie Mullins, gal orchestra leader. There was a fine organ there, but no organist was featured. During the second show, which started at five o'clock, Fats would take over the organ.[21]

John Hammond (right) recalls the early days in Harlem with trumpeter Buck Clayton at Clayton's 70th birthday party.

The place would have been more or less empty at the time when Fats started playing. Gradually – despite the hour – Fats attracted a following of his own. The owner, Mrs Marie Downs, took Fats on to the staff at a salary which the *New York Times* reported in his obituary as being $23 a week.[22]

As a young jazz fan, John Hammond used to stand outside the Lincoln at this period, when he too was only in his early teens. "I would listen outside because Fats Waller was playing organ there. He played for the silent movies, often injecting his own off-beat riffs, to the amusement of the audience."[23] Hammond was too scared to go into the theater alone. Theater historian Ted Fox has pointed out that during this period the Lincoln was one of only two Harlem movie houses catering mainly for African-American audiences (the other was the Crescent). Otherwise Harlem theaters were strictly segregated; those which admitted African-Americans – such as the Alhambra – had separate entrances. Because the Harlem theaters virtually all changed their policies during the 1920s, it is necessary to think back to the pre-1920 period as one when the Lincoln stood more or less alone in offering an opportunity for a young musician like Fats to emerge from the audience and play for his own community.

Elsewhere, only the galleries were reserved for African-Americans, and attracted the term "nigger heaven" (later adopted for his book about Harlem by Carl Van Vechten). It was a remarkable combination of coincidence that the young Waller should have had easy access to so few theaters, but that one of the two open to him happened to have an organ; not all Harlem theaters were so equipped.

Fats's appearances at the Lincoln were attended not just by his classmates from high school, but also by other budding young African-American musicians. Unlike John Hammond, members of the African-American community felt no danger in entering the theater and enjoyed Fats's playing from inside. Since the mid-1960s the building that was the Lincoln, at the corner of 135th Street and Lenox Avenue, has been a church; white-painted and respectable, it gives little hint of its past.

The bandleader and arranger Don Redman was one of those to whom the sight of the church brought back old memories. "This is where I first became good friends with the wonderful Fats Waller. I used to sit on the organ bench with him listening as he played for the silent movies."[24]

By far the most important of Fats's organ-bench colleagues was Count Basie. Like Fats, Basie was in awe of the theater's $10,000 Wurlitzer pipe organ. Once invited up to the bench with Waller, the young Bill Basie was shown how to operate the pedals. He began by playing the bass parts with his feet in accompaniment to Waller, but once the Count had mastered the difficult art of playing a bass line without looking down at his feet, Fats invited him to take over the manuals (keyboards) too. The instrument had two manuals (bigger Wurlitzers had up to four), and Waller showed the young Basie how to set up different combinations of pipes (registrations) on each keyboard so that one was effectively the "solo" part, and the other the "accompaniment." This remained the basis of Waller's organ style. All his recordings on organ show his penchant for contrasting tone colors on different manuals – a technique he was to continue on the new Hammond electric organ (invented in 1933) with its greater percussive possibilities.

There are relatively few organists in the history of jazz, and it is significant that two of the greatest, Waller and Basie, enjoyed a master–pupil relationship in the early 1920s. Fortunately, Waller left a considerable body of recordings on both pipe and Hammond organ, but Basie has a far smaller legacy. On the few tunes where it is possible to compare their work, it is clear that Basie's style owes much to Fats's influence. (Other jazz organists from the 1920s and 1930s include Milt Herth, who made some strange recordings with Willie "the Lion" Smith and the drummer O'Neill Spencer, and Glenn Hardman, who made some recordings with members of Basie's orchestra.)

Waller was unique among jazz organists of his period in that all his recordings suggest he found the registrational possibilities of the instrument to be an extension of the vocabulary of jazz improvisation. This aspect of his work was largely overlooked until the 1980s, but is excellently analyzed in Paul Machlin's book *Stride*, which is the first detailed attempt to investigate Waller's playing in terms of conventional music analysis.

The Lincoln, like other Harlem theaters, had its own conventions and characters. Basie encountered most of them – especially since, once Fats had "broken him in," Basie found himself taking over at the keyboard while Fats continued a pressing engagement with a card game backstage. While Mrs Downs ran her theater with a firm control, the stage acts that ran between the films were organized by Pip, the manager, who decided which acts stayed in after the week's first show. No publicity photos went up for the week until after the first house, and then only those for the acts that satisfied the rigorous standards of the stage manager. A regular performer was Cephus, a whistler, whom

Basie found himself accompanying in place of Fats, and who had trained the audience to join in on various familiar phrases. Their enthusiastic response always made his act go over well.

From the base of the Lincoln, and later the Lafayette, Fats established himself as the leading African-American theater organist. Nevertheless, throughout his life and career, he did not lose sight of the origins of his interest in the organ. The Rev. Adam Clayton Powell (pastor of the Abyssinian Baptist Church in Harlem, at which the Waller family worshiped) recalled: "through the years, he had open invitations to use the great organ of the church when available. Oft times in the middle of the day, or late at night, Fats would come to church, sit at the great four-manual Moller, and play negro spirituals, the old gospel songs."

For most of his life, Fats was enchanted by the organ – whether the church- or theater-sized concert instrument, or the portable Hammond organ that he later used as a regular part of his act. He attracted the admiration of organists and keyboard players everywhere for his use of the instrument, and many of the clubs at which he was to have residencies in the later stages of his career installed an organ especially for him.

The $23 a week that Fats was bringing home in 1920 from his employment at the Lincoln was a good start. But it quickly became inadequate for his needs, since late in that year Waller married Edith Hatchett, moving in with her and her parents at an apartment in the Bronx. Fats had met her at a party near her Brook Avenue home while playing with a pick-up band some time before the death of Adeline Waller, his mother. Now, away from his own family home, he plunged into an early marriage which, it became more and more evident as time went by, was a mistake.

At first, things went well, and Fats cut down on the party circuit and the bar crawling which had become his way of life. But the financial demands of his wife and the news that a baby was on the way sent him back to the clubs in search of work as a pianist, hoping to bolster the modest income from the Lincoln Theater. After the birth of Thomas Jr. in the spring of 1921, Fats was away from home even more. Despite moving to their own apartment, away from the Hatchett parents, the pressures on the couple were too great: Edith was not disposed to put up with the life of a musician's wife. By 1923 they were separated, and subsequently divorced. Fats was expected to pay alimony on a regular basis, and this was the root of constant problems for him for almost all the remainder of his life. He was late with payments, or forgot about them altogether as he went away from home, and the frequent appearances of process servers and bailiffs became as much a part of the Waller legend as the drink and the vast meals.

Despite the collapse of his marriage, his keyboard playing went from strength to strength. During the period from 1920 to 1923, the tutelage of James P. Johnson paid off, and Fats became fully established as one of the major Harlem pianists, a recording artist, and the maker of piano rolls.

As a rent party pianist, he got on to the circuit organized by Lippy Boyette, and took his place alongside most of the other Harlem players. Maurice Waller and Ed Kirkeby both allude to the surprise with which Russell Brooks and others among the slightly older players responded to hearing the marked improvement in Fats's playing after his stint as a pupil of James P.

Fats was capable of learning from the other giants too. Luckey Roberts remembers Fats relieving him as house pianist at Barron Wilkins's club (owned and operated by the brother of the owner of Leroy's) and how he taught Fats various techniques for "certain chords and ... special effects." Roberts was impressed with the young Waller: "Every note stood out sharp and clear, and there was no blurring and slurring as some sloppy performers would do. ... He owned a pair of fast hands with great power that allowed him to do things beyond the range of the ordinary pianist."[25]

Fats's first recordings were made in 1922: a pair of piano solos issued back to back on the Okeh label (4757), and entitled *Muscle Shoals Blues* and *Birmingham Blues*. The conventional dating for these is October 21, 1922, but it is possible (argues Brian Rust, on the basis of the matrix and take numbers) that they were recorded as late as December the same year. In 1923, Waller's first piano roll, *Got to Cool My Doggies Now*, was issued, followed the same year by nine or ten more.

Piano rolls were the method by which Waller first started to learn the stride style at the Brooks household. His own rolls demonstrate, by following his own methods of stopping the mechanism for close analysis of the fingering, just how advanced Waller's technique was by this time. Operated by a sympathetic performer, Fats's piano rolls give a more vivid impression than do his early records of how he must have sounded in 1923. Paul Machlin has charted the release dates of the piano rolls in his recording chronology, and although these are not directly linked to recording dates, it is evident that the rolls appeared in a steady sequence during the year. The entire surviving output from these rolls has been recorded and was released on LP by the

Fats at the organ.

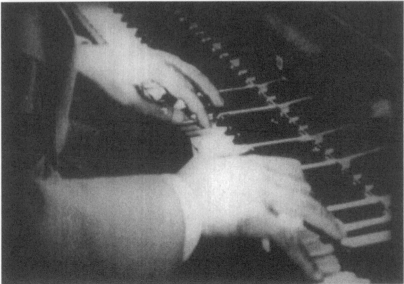

The hands of Waller, striding at the keyboard, showing his full stretch. In the first photograph his left little finger is playing the bass note on the first beat of the bar, doubling the "backward tenth" with his left thumb. In the second, he is on the second beat of the bar, grouping a chord around his left thumb, which carries the countermelody.

Biograph company in three volumes of their Piano Roll Series, with the 1910 player piano operated by Michael Montgomery.

Analyzing the publicity for the QRS company piano rolls is instructive concerning the place of the player piano in American society, and about the well-developed business of advertising and direct-mail selling in the American press as early as the mid-1920s. A large advertisement for QRS appeared in the *Chicago Defender* for August 18, 1923, which makes clear that QRS had set up a special division, comparable with the "race" catalogs of the big recording companies, for presenting the music of black artists to African-American people:

> Some time since, the QRS company announced the addition of a special department, through which the characteristic music of the Negro Race would be made available for the player piano and recorded by artists of their own people, thus insuring accurate interpretations. A still greater success of this department is now assured by special arrangements recently made with additional Negro Artists, and the company is pleased to make the following announcement!

It then goes on to list Lemuel Fowler, J. Lawrence Cook, Clarence Williams, Clarence Johnson, and Luckyeth Roberts, not to mention the young Thomas Waller, and – in pride of place – James P. Johnson. Each is photographed in vignette, above the legend "These seven well known Negro Composer-pianists have been added to the QRS corps of recording artists, thereby insuring for its patrons a larger variety of unquestioned interpretations of negro music on player rolls."

Waller's *Haitian Blues* is billed as the "Latest Blues Sensation," and at the bottom of the panel there is a request to customers to enrol on the mailing list for the QRS bulletin, which gives a monthly list of new issues. The business methods of subscriber selling have not changed much today.

It is significant that the advertisement refers to player-composers, since many of the piano roll pieces were Fats's own compositions.

Before his twentieth birthday, in addition to securing a reputation as a pianist and organist, Fats was established in the third major area of his musical career. As he spread his wings to encompass songwriting as well as composing solo piano pieces in the stride tradition, Fats became a familiar figure in the music publishers' offices in Broadway. It was here that he joined all the hopefuls selling their songs for a cash advance against royalties that might never come, or (as Fats more frequently and inadvisedly did) signing away the copyrights outright for a fee.

In this fast-moving world of Tin Pan Alley, a major part of the Waller legend grew up. The stories of Fats selling songs for $10 apiece, or trading them for hamburgers with Fletcher Henderson, or parting with lucrative royalty contracts for a minuscule cash advance covering a total assignment of rights, are legion, and it is virtually impossible to separate the fact from the fiction.[26]

Fats collaborated with a number of different lyric writers, as well as co-composers. His main lyricist over the years was Andy Razaf. Razaf was a brilliant and witty verbal craftsman, who had a romantic legend attached to him, in that he claimed to be the son of the Duke of Madagascar, who had been killed when the French overran the island, his mother having been able to escape to Washington, DC, where he was born. Andy rejoiced in the full name of Andreamentena Razafinkeriefo.[27]

Razaf recalled the partnership for *Metronome* in 1944: "One of the first things we did was to cash in on a vogue for West Indian songs. As soon as we got broke, all we had to do was grind out two or three West Indian numbers, take them up to Mills, or some Broadway office, and get a nice sum for them." Andy also remembered that he and Fats had continued to work in the *Boy in a Boat* vein. "Around that time there was a heavy demand for cabaret-type songs with blue lyrics. We did hundreds of those."[28]

Soon, according to Harry Dial, Fats's drummer from the 1930s, "Fats had quite an income from all those songs he had written. You could always go down to ASCAP and get an advance on next year's royalties. Because soon Fats was in the top bracket." Although Fats was often careless, or (as Razaf implies) would make for the Broadway publishers' offices in search of a fast buck, when he chose to look after his business properly he could make quite a reasonable amount for his songs. "He was getting big money for those days," remembered Harry Dial. "There was a gang of them would hang out together. There was James P. Johnson, who was Fats's teacher, there was J. C. Johnson, Alex Hill, Andy Razaf, and Fats. Almost always when you'd see one of them, you'd see the others. All of them drinkers. Even James P. was a drinker in that company."[29] And while Harry's views must be taken as a combination of hearsay and his experiences from the 1930s, when he arrived in New York, he gives a vivid picture of the group of songwriters in whose company Fats lived and worked.

The social environment in which Waller found himself in the early and mid-1920s was effectively a complete cross-section of New York life. At one level, he was working in the Harlem after-hours clubs and even in the whorehouses. (His *Valentine Stomp* is a tribute to one of Harlem's most famous "madames.") He was playing the theater organ for fun, the church organ for spiritual and physical relaxation. He was turning out songs for Tin Pan Alley. He was an increasingly frequent visitor to the recording studios as blues accompanist, soloist, and, as time went by, band pianist. He was cutting piano rolls regularly. Although he was gradually abandoning the rent party circuit by the mid-1920s, he had been adopted by the whites who had "discovered" African-American Harlem, who hired him to play at parties for the well-to-do in downtown Manhattan and in the fashionable apartments of Riverside Drive. At these parties, he is rumored to have rubbed shoulders with George Gershwin and other members of New York's musical and theatrical life.

It was at this time that he is supposed to have studied (either in New York or Chicago) with the famous concert pianist Leopold Godowsky. Although the Lithuanian-born Godowsky had taught in Chicago before World War I, he followed a relatively nomadic existence in the period between his return to the USA in 1918 and the stroke that ended his playing career in 1930. During the 1920s he toured Europe, South America, and Asia extensively, but when at home in New York or Chicago, Godowsky surrounded himself with friends and musicians from all walks of life. He preferred to perform in the intimate surroundings of his apartment than in the concert hall, and gave his last public American recital as early as 1922. His friend Abram Chasins wrote: "No musician was more capable of constantly gathering around him creative companions in so many fields of artistic work."[30] Godowsky was a frequent visitor to the well-to-do party circuit on which Fats, James P., and the Lion played regularly. There is no evidence to support claims made in Waller's press releases, and later in interviews, that he studied formally with Godowsky. An article from the *Pittsburgh Courier* of February 1, 1936 includes one of the earliest such assertions to find its way into print, saying of the pianist that "he studied under Godowsky of Vienna and Carl Bohn [*sic*] of New York." In October 1938, in an interview between Waller and Nils Hellström, the editor of the Swedish jazz magazine *Orkester Journalen*, Fats claimed that

> he had studied piano in Vienna around 1920. He arrived there with his friend and trombone player Herbert Flemming, and another boy who was playing violin. All the three boys were not more than fifteen years old and the teacher was very severe towards them. Fats got so many hits on his fingers he barely managed the scales, and the violinist got his violin banged on his head, and the violin was broken in smithereens.[31]

Such an account is so fanciful, not least the idea that boys who had traveled to a different continent to study music would be treated in so crude a fashion, that it seems extraordinary that it was taken seriously. Furthermore, it would appear that Fats was somewhat confused about the origins of his two apparent mentors. The Austrian conductor Karl Böhm was the one of the pair who had connections with Vienna, as he worked with the city's Symphony Orchestra from 1933, and became head of the Staatsoper there the following year, but he did not make his New York debut until fourteen years after Waller's death, when he conducted *Don Giovanni* at the Metropolitan Opera. Godowsky, by contrast, had nothing to do with Vienna, but he was a highly respected piano teacher in both New York and Chicago. Having grown up near Vilnius in Lithuania, Godowsky studied in Berlin, before first coming to the USA in his teens as a touring piano soloist. Not long before Waller's birth he had held appointments at New York's College of Music and the Chicago Conservatory as head of piano, and although he then spent many years in Europe, he was back in the USA by the time Waller was fifteen, and was once more touring and teaching until he retired from the concert platform. Many of the extant biographies of Waller, and countless liner notes, nevertheless accept Waller's remarks at face value. I remain unclear about any connection he may have had with Böhm, or why he should have plucked this particular name out of the air, but I am reasonably certain that Waller was one of the crowd of "creative companions" sought by Godowsky, and that they would have encountered one another on the social round where Fats was employed as an entertainer. The degree of "teacher–pupil" relationship possible in those circumstances is difficult to ascertain.

Whatever the truth of Waller's classical studies with Godowsky (and others), by the mid-1920s he was well established as a pianist and songwriter, as an organist and accompanist, and (although he had not at that stage started to sing himself) as a Harlem character. But the world of Manhattan was too small to contain Waller for long. The lure of vaudeville and the theater introduced him to new horizons. By the end of the decade he had made an impact not merely as a songwriter, but also as the author of a string of major hits.

THE MUSICAL
THEATER

Most of Fats Waller's career in the musical theater took place in a very brief period, between 1926, when he collaborated on the scores for *Tan Town Topics* and *Junior Blackbirds* with Spencer Williams, and 1929, when he wrote *Hot Chocolates* with Andy Razaf. It was not until shortly before his death in 1943 that he began writing for the stage again, with the show *Early to Bed*. In the late 1920s, Waller's stage work was not restricted to writing shows, since he also directed pit bands and appeared as an accompanist for singers. Mostly he specialized in the genre of African-American revue. The floorshows at many Harlem clubs were a curious admixture of comedy sketches, dancing, and singing, and the borderline between them and the vaudeville shows that toured the TOBA (Theater Owners' Booking Agency – or "Tough on Black Asses") circuit of African-American theaters was almost non-existent. Indeed, there are plenty of not too apocryphal stories of floorshows put on by black singers and dancers in front of white club audiences being performed again the same evening in African-American or mixed theaters for black audiences. Fats's own show *Hot Chocolates* became one of these.

The chronology of Waller's involvement with the stage is

Garvin Bushell (right)
with Gene Sedric: two
of Waller's reedmen
together.

confused. But if his career as a theater organist is discounted, then we
can reckon that his tour with Liza and her Shufflin' Six marks his debut
as a vaudeville accompanist. In his study of Fats's music, Paul Machlin
gives 1921 as the date for this tour, but this is probably a conclusion
drawn from the two standard biographies by Ed Kirkeby and Maurice
Waller. These refer to "a short tour with a burlesque show," which they
date as 1921, the summer after Thomas Waller Jr. was born, and after
Fats's visit as solo pianist to Scotty's Bar, over the river in New Jersey.

In fact, the tour took place in 1923.[1] Garvin Bushell, the clarinet
and saxophone player, recalled having been a member of this group
when he spoke to Nat Hentoff for the *Jazz Review*.

> Until October 1923 I was part of a vaudeville act – Modern
> Cocktail ... that went to the west coast and back ... I then
> went with Adams and Robinson. Clarence Robinson, who was

a fine singer and dancer, and I finally took the act over and the
pianist was Fats Waller. He'd been playing the organ at the
Lincoln Theatre on 135th and Leonox [sic] Avenue, and I
asked him to join us. He was still a big kid; he used to come
into the theatre with an apple on a stick. The act was called
Liza (she was Katie Crippen) and Her Shuffling Sextet. When
Robinson and I split up, I took over the band, including Fats
and Katie.[2]

Subsequently, Garvin Bushell recalled further memories of this
tour in a conversation with Mark Tucker in July 1986.

Clarence [Robinson] wanted to have "Clarence and the Band."
We said, "No, no, no. Let's have something with another
name." Then we got Katie in there, and one of the agents
downtown thought up Liza and Her Shuffling Sextet. That's
the way it was.

There was Fats, Lou, Seymour, myself, Mert, that's five,
Clarence was six. . . . We had various dancers. We had Arthur
Bryson, we had another guy. Then we finally had Bill Basie on
piano. He came with us, the latter part of the act, before the
act broke up. Before Seymour was killed. Seymour, our
trumpet player, was shot in Johnny Hudgins's house. A girl
shot him. He had a room at Johnny Hudgins's up in the South
Bronx, and this girl shot Seymour. She didn't get a day. The
judge acquitted her and she went back to Pennsylvania. [She
was] a white girl.

We weren't playing the TOBA circuit. We were playing big
time vaudeville! No, I got to remind you, Adams and Robinson
were a big time headline act. And they put the band in their
act. They never were a TOBA act like Sissle and Blake. They
were big time. So we played the Keith and Loews circuit.
Pantages. Keith. Like the same circuit that the Modern
Cocktail played. Neither of those acts ever played the black
circuit at all. Liza and the Shufflin' Sextet was the same thing.

Fats wasn't a composer then. Fats hadn't composed anything

then. He was not seen opening his mouth. He drank as much,
but he didn't sing. We didn't know he could sing. We would
have had him singing. He was just playing a whole lot of piano.
We considered him a piano player and that's it.[3]

Tucker went on to ask Garvin about the social life of the band.
They would, it seems, go out on the town after the show. From this,
we get a picture of the self-esteem of the "big time" vaudeville band,
and a little more insight into the lifestyle of the touring circuit after
hours.

Sure, we'd go to a nightclub, and pick up chicks and all that. I
don't remember being with Fats on any of these occasions, but
Mert Perry and I were always together. Seymour was so erratic.
He was an erratic Geechie. He had a good philosophy and he
was a pinchpenny. All he talked about was money. Very
immaculate. He kept himself clean, dressed well. Matter of fact,
everybody in that group, dressing was their big act, and we
smoked big cigars – La Preferentiale, Madeira. Mert set the
standard. He was a cocky little guy, like a little banty rooster.
But he was immaculate and sharp and very sophisticated, very
articulate.[4]

Count Basie was fairly certain that there was another pianist who
worked with Katie Crippen between Fats and himself. By the time
Basie was with them she called the act "Katie Krippen and her
Kiddies." When Basie played for her (and Albert Murray, the co-author
of Basie's autobiography dates this 1924–5) Mert Perry was still on
drums, the late Seymour had been replaced by Freddie Douglas, and he
recalls Elmer Williams on saxophone.

"It was mainly her act. She sang and danced, and Lou Henry, who
was her husband, played the trombone and was the unit manager and
musical director."

Basie describes how an African-American act came to be touring
the major "Columbia Wheel" theater circuit. Katie's group was the only

African-American ensemble to be featured. They played between the first and second parts of the main show, which had a chorus line, a show band, two comedians, and – the prerequisite of a burlesque show – a "prima donna stripper."

"Our act . . . was a special feature that used to be called the olio. We didn't have any connection with the skits and production numbers or anything like that. We came on and did our thing and that was it."[5]

It is possible to get something of an impression of how Katie Crippen's band might have sounded from the four sides she recorded for the Black Swan record company in 1921. Bushell is on the second two sides together with Buster Bailey on clarinet and saxes, and the pianist Willie Gant (although the band was under Fletcher Henderson's name he seems not to have played piano himself on these sides). *Blind Man Blues* is typical – Crippen telling her story forcefully of how she "came up from Tennessee" with the band playing a simple, skeletal arrangement behind her. It is probable that although she was being backed by a mixture of New York studio players and her own regular group, this type of loose-limbed ensemble, with the reeds occasionally stepping out of the *mêlée* to imitate one of her phrases or emphasize a passing harmony, is close to how she sounded on the touring circuits with Waller in the line-up.

Equally, it is possible to get a flavor of Fats's accompanimental style at precisely this period since he recorded two tracks with the blues singer Sara Martin on November 1, 1923. It is highly likely that these were made just before the tour with Liza and her Shufflin' Sextet, and in contrast to Waller's first records with Martin (made a year earlier in December 1922) the 1923 sides have her teamed up as a vocal duo with Clarence Williams. There is more than a hint of vaudeville in their *Squabbling Blues* (OK 8108).

During 1924 and 1925 Fats is not reported to have indulged in any further burlesque or vaudeville tours. He did, however, cut a number of discs with singers who were experienced in the world of African-American theater, including Alberta Hunter and Ethel Waters. There are rumors that he also undertook a tour with Bessie Smith; and the discovery in 2000 of a picture of Waller with Smith's backing band may substantiate this. He is known to have continued to frequent Harlem nightspots as a pianist and socializer, and to have been featured opposite Duke Ellington's band at the Kentucky Club (off Seventh Avenue at Times Square) as "Ali Baba – The Egyptian Wonder" in 1925. This was largely through the good offices of a Capt. George H. Maines, who was a Broadway press agent with a taste for Waller's style of piano playing (and hokum). Maines was instrumental in getting the entire Kentucky Club show booked in for a one-night appearance at the downtown New Amsterdam Theater, on the theater's dark night (the one night a week when its regular show was not playing). According to Maurice Waller the show ran there one night a week for two months.[6]

In May 1925, Waller was featured playing the organ, and as part of a small band, in the first African-American vaudeville show to be presented at the Lafayette by Frank Schiffman (who had also by then taken over the Lincoln Theater from Marie Downs). Schiffman at one time or another owned most of the African-American theaters in Harlem, and is perhaps best known for his lifetime enterprise, the Apollo. By presenting vaudeville at the Lafayette, he was reviving the traditions that had been established there earlier in the 1920s by previous managements. Jackson's *Billboard* column, for instance, noted that at one point in 1923 three floorshows were running there concurrently. In the early 1920s, the singer Bricktop had come to fame there in shows directed by Allie Ross.

According to Maurice Waller, following a spell at the Sherman Hotel in Chicago in 1925, Fats returned to New York. The following year he made his first major contribution as a composer for the stage by writing songs (with Spencer Williams) for a show at the Lafayette called *Tan Town Topics*. In common with other Harlem theaters, the Lafayette put on short-run shows for three or four weeks apiece. Some then went on to make a short tour of East Coast African-American theaters, but even including this the maximum run for any of these shows was about six weeks.

Among the main Harlem theaters active in the mid-1920s was the Harlem Opera House, at 209 West 125th Street, owned by Schiffman and Brecher from about 1922. There was the Lafayette, at 2227 Seventh Avenue at 131st Street, also owned from 1925 by Schiffman and Brecher, which had put on several shows by James P. Johnson, including *Plantation Days* and *Raisin' Cain* in 1923 and *Moochin' Along* in 1925. At 58 West 135th Street was the Lincoln Theater. This had been built in 1909 by Mrs Marie Downs, and rebuilt by her as a much larger theater on the same site in 1915. Schiffman took the Lincoln over in the early 1920s.

Brecher also owned the Odeon on 145th Street, the Roosevelt at 145th and Fifth Avenue, and the Douglas at 142nd and Lenox Avenue, and he operated Loew's Seventh Avenue on 124th Street. His principal competitor was Gosdorfer, who ran the Alhambra on Seventh Avenue and 126th Street until it folded in 1931.

In contrast with the theaters on the TOBA circuit, the Lafayette was one of the more upmarket theaters across the Eastern states which got together to coordinate bookings and to establish the rates for principal performers. The others were the Royal, Baltimore; the Howard, Washington, D.C.; and the Earle in Philadelphia. Danny Barker recalled touring these houses during the mid-1930s with the Mills Blue Rhythm Orchestra under Lucky Millinder. Irving Mills typified the kind of promoter with whom the theater managements set their rates and coordinated the booking of their acts. Mills beat them at their own game. If they wanted Duke Ellington, that would be fine, but in order to have Duke in two, maybe three, months' time, well, they'd just have to book Lucky Millinder and the Blue Rhythm Orchestra round the entire circuit this month. By employing these tactics and holding out the offer of his two or three really major performers, Mills was able to keep several acts in work. It was a policy that later suited other promoters, such as Armstrong's manager, Joe Glaser.

As well as the Harlem theaters, there were the nightclubs and dance halls. These were described in the *Melody Maker* during

November 1929 by Edgar Jackson: "Connie's and the Cotton Club and Smalls' are show places catering for the visitor desiring to see the sights. More obscure and more interesting are the small clubs where white people are not encouraged." Broadly speaking, clubs in the former category, which also included the Plantation, the Kentucky Club (before the opening of the Cotton Club), and Barron Wilkins's Club (until the proprietor was murdered in the mid-1920s), were capable of mounting big floorshows equivalent to those staged in Harlem's vaudeville theaters.

By contrast, the after-hours joints seldom had more than a solo pianist or a small house band, and often catered for the performers from the bigger clubs and theaters looking for places to relax after work. Fats Waller frequented both sizes of club, as performer and barfly, and he also visited the dance halls – the Arcadia (downtown at 53rd Street on Broadway), the Roseland (catering for a white audience, but featuring African-American orchestras such as Fletcher Henderson's, and located at 51st and Broadway), and the Savoy (opened in 1926) at 596 Lenox Avenue.

The songs that Fats wrote for the 1926 Lafayette show, *Tan Town Topics*, included the hit *Señorita Mine*. A number of other songs copyrighted that year by various permutations of the same team of Waller, Eddie Rector, and Spencer and Clarence Williams probably also emanate from Fats's stage work. These include *Charleston Hound*, *That Struttin' Eddie of Mine*, *Crazy 'bout That Man I Love*, *Old Folks Shuffle*, and *Midnight Stomp*.

The exact chronology and content of *Tan Town Topics* is obscure, but it is known that Fats wrote the score for a second show in 1926, which was called *Junior Blackbirds* in imitation of the Lew Leslie hit *Blackbirds of 1926*. Owing to his habit of selling tunes for ready money, the publication of Fats's songs is so confused an area that it is impossible to identify from date of publication or copyright details exactly which tunes were in the two shows (except for *Charleston Hound*, which is known to have been part of *Tan Town Topics*). We know from surviving programs and reviews of his later stage works

The Apollo Theater, the flagship in the group of theaters owned by Schiffman and Brecher, and run by them from 1934.

that the content of each show changed radically during a run. The vaudeville element of the Lafayette pieces was such that the needs of individual performers led to a constant process of adaptation. Fats's stage director for both revues was Leonard Harper, with whom he was later to work on the shows written for Connie's Inn, and for whom Waller played in a production called *Creole Follies*, in July 1926. Harper (like the other directors of the shows at the Lafayette) would have been responsible, together with the manager Schiffman, for deciding on the final form of the revues, and for the changes that took place during the run. Schiffman developed his instincts for what would go over well with an African-American audience into a fine art. Later, as manager of the Apollo, he kept the theater in the forefront of New York African-American entertainment for many years. Schiffman, even as early in his career as the Lafayette period, was famous for the way in which he dealt with acts that were not successful. Performers knew that a short word of encouragement was good news, but they dreaded his embrace. An arm around the shoulders and a confidential chat was a widely recognized code that the act was to be dropped from the show.

At some point between or after the two Lafayette shows, Waller was featured in a revue at the Lincoln with "Signor Fats Waller's Lincolnians", which ran from July 17 to 23, 1926. He also began sitting in with Fletcher Henderson's popular big band, downtown at the Roseland Ballroom. This culminated in Fats making some discs as a guest with that orchestra late in 1926.

The next short period of Fats's life, from the end of 1926 to early 1928 and the opening of his first major stage success, *Keep Shufflin'*, included three significant events. He remarried, he began his recording association with Victor, and he spent a period in Chicago.

Anita Waller (*née* Rutherford) was to have a sobering effect on the more wayward side of Fats's character, although the second marriage (which some accounts suggest remained a common-law arrangement) intensified Waller's problems over alimony payments to his first wife, Edith. Wrapped up in his new relationship (but still dedicated to

Anita Rutherford.

having a good time), Waller was all too often to forget his obligations to his former wife and to Thomas Jr. He also moved from the Bronx, where his former wife lived, back to Harlem.

The Victor association brought a greater degree of stability to Waller, too. In the pre-Depression period up to 1929, when the American record industry was at its height, it was helpful to any musician's career to have a big recording association with a company such as Victor. And so, in the *Chicago Defender* for January 29, 1927, we find a glowing accolade for Waller's recent Victor pipe-organ recording of *St. Louis Blues* and *Lenox Avenue Blues*:

"New Orthophonic Victor Records! A Sensation!!!"

"Fats Waller makes this pipe organ 'Croon the blues.'"

The disc cost 75 cents, the standard for a 10-inch record on the "race" catalog.

Coverage in the *Defender* was good for another reason, too. It helped spread the word to the Chicago audience about the new acts to appear in town, and to a national readership about who was doing what. The African-American press in the USA at this time was a curious combination of local newspaper and national "underground" press for African-American people. As Danny Barker said in an interview with the author:

"I checked on who were the great bands, the great musicians . . . you would read about [them] in the *Amsterdam News* in New York; the *New York Age*; the *Chicago Defender*, which was published nationally . . . and later on came the *Pittsburgh Courier*."[7]

Fats set off for Chicago after a busy period in the studios. He had completed his first recordings with Fletcher Henderson's big band (November 1926) and made eight further organ solos and one piano solo (on January 14, and February 16, 1927). He had been featured organist at the Lincoln Theater during the time that these sessions took place.[8] Both Ed Kirkeby and Maurice Waller suggest that the Chicago trip was in May 1927, but in fact by May, Fats was back in New York. This can be confirmed by reference to the string of articles and advertisements in the *Chicago Defender* that accompanied Fats's visit.

The first mention is a small editorial piece in the issue of March 12, 1927:

> Fats Waller, the organist from New York, has been retained to play the mammoth pipe organ in the Vendome Theater. He comes direct from the Lincoln Theater, New York where he was a sensation. With this great organist and Erskine Tate's orchestra it will give the Vendome Theater the distinction of being the most delightful theater catering to race patronage in the United States.[9]

There is no doubt that the Vendome in the 1920s was to Chicago what the Apollo was to become to New York in the 1930s and 1940s. The Vendome ran movies, it had Tate's band, which was one of the greatest in Chicago, and it also presented "Stage Specialties." It was run by Hammond and Sons, a management concern that had started in Chicago's theater district around 1919. The March 12 *Defender* tells us:

Victor's advertisement from January 29, 1927.

[They] opened a little 250 seat house on Indiana Avenue at 31st Street, and called it the Elba Theater, using all of their capital to put it over. Finally a success, they bought the Little Grand Theater from Duke Brannon, H. A. Ingalls and Gen. H. Smith. Naming it the Phoenix, they gave the public the best in pictures of those days, and today the Vendome Theater is the crowning glory of their efforts.

Nor were Hammond and Sons unsure of their market. All their publicity was aimed at "the race": "Hammond and Sons are giving the public sincere returns for their patronage. They are giving the best that the market affords because they have the Race at heart. It is not 'get the money' only with them. They are proud of the Vendome Theater and its patrons."

There is plenty of evidence that the Hammonds stuck to their word, especially as the featured trumpet soloist with Tate's orchestra from December 1925 until about the end of Fats's visit in April 1927 was Louis Armstrong. Armstrong doubled, by appearing later each night with Carroll Dickerson's orchestra, at the Sunset Café.

From Armstrong's biographer James Lincoln Collier we can get the outline of the proceedings at the Vendome (which was situated at State Street and 32nd Street). "The show usually opened with Erskine Tate's 'Little Symphony' playing an overture. Then followed the movie, and at intermission Tate's 'Jazz Syncopators' would play a hot feature. Armstrong played not only solos during the jazz number, but frequently an operatic air or standard solo piece."[10]

There were three changes of movie each week. One played from Monday to Wednesday, another from Wednesday to Saturday, and there was a special showing on Sundays. Fats was required to accompany the silent movies in much the same way as he had done in New York as theater organist at the Lincoln and Lafayette. The policy of the theater was to present "first-run" motion pictures. We can get an impression of the programs by looking at the bill for the first two weeks of Fats's engagement. During the first, starting on Thursday

March 24, 1927, the main feature was Ronald Colman in *The Winning of Barbara Worth*. Then came Bebe Daniels in *A Kiss in a Taxi*, and finally Corinne Griffith in *The Lady in Ermine*. The following week was something of a Joan Crawford feature – she starred in *The Understanding Heart* and later in *The Taxi Dancer*, the intervening picture being *Blind Alleys* with Thomas Meighan.

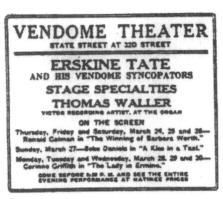

One of the things this shows is that there were no special concessions to the African-American audience in the choice of picture, since the films were all standard Hollywood output and not specially made for the "Race" audience. The stage and pit-band shows were the part of the Vendome presentation that appealed particularly to the public the Hammonds were after. There was a matinée every day and a full evening performance, before the performers (like Armstrong) scurried off to fit in another gig. The advertisements all promised: "Come before 6.30 pm and see the entire evening performance at Matinee prices." And already, following hard on the heels of the release of his first Victor sides, the Vendome ads billed Waller as "Victor Recording Artist."[11]

Indeed, it wasn't long before Victor were doing the theater a reciprocal favor, and as the advertisements came out for the next two couplings of Waller organ solos they proclaimed "THOMAS WALLER, popular organist, is now playing at the Vendome Theater in Chicago." The sides, *Rusty Pail Blues*, *Sloppy Water Blues*, *Soothin' Syrup*, and *Loveless Love*, had been recorded in Camden, New Jersey, on January

14, 1927, and were advertised in the Victor new records panel in the *Defender* on April 16. This gives an interesting insight into the lead times for pressing and releasing a single in the race catalog.

The Chicago movie houses employed all manner of public relations gambits to lure in audiences. To some extent the films were secondary to the live entertainment at the Vendome, and when the theater came to present Lon Chaney's *Tell It to the Marines* (April 18–20, 1927), the billing concentrated on Tate and Waller. The rival Metropolitan Theater, run by Ascher's and featuring a stage show with Blanche Calloway, was not content to rely on Miss Calloway, her Six Easter Buds, and Sammy Stewart's orchestra to pull in audiences for the same film. And so, on Wednesday the 20th, Ascher's announced that they were mounting a special event: "Company A of the Eighth Regiment I.N.G. in Flag Raising ceremonies, Wednesday April 20 at 7.30 pm in honor of Lon Chaney in 'Tell it to the Marines.'"

Waller left at the beginning of May 1927. He was detained by police to do with unpaid alimony, which hastened his departure.[12] He was back in the recording studio with Henderson in New York on the 11th. The Vendome presumably reverted to Tate's band playing behind the movies, as it had done before Waller's arrival. The young Earl Hines, Carroll Dickerson's pianist, recalled that he had taken over Teddy Weatherford's chair with Tate, playing with the band behind the movie. "[Tate] used to get script and music sent him with the film. There would be several themes about eight or sixteen bars long, which were used for changes of scene, as when a door closed and the characters went outside." Hines went on to recall that Tate employed a code, by holding up various fingers, to indicate to his men which of the short musical excerpts they should play next: "If he held out his fourth finger it meant they had to go to the fourth theme for, say, cloudiness in the sky, and to get ready for a rough section of the music."[13]

Hines also remembered that during the Vendome engagement Fats would come and sit in with the band at the Sunset Café. According to Hines, Carroll Dickerson had recently been sacked for drinking, and

Earl himself had taken over the band. To allow Hines to conduct and to rehearse the routines, the band had taken on a full-time second pianist, Willie Hamby. Fats would come and sit in at Hamby's piano and play alongside Hines. The Sunset band was a particularly fine one at this period, with not only Hines and Armstrong, but also the fine New Orleans drummer Tubby Hall and the trumpeter Natty Dominique. Joe Oliver's former trombonist Honoré Dutrey was also featured. It would have been very splendid to hear this group with the added dynamism of Waller at the piano.

The details surrounding Waller's return to New York are sketchy, apart from a sole Chicago press report that he was in police custody. According to Kirkeby, Waller had to return to New York as a consequence of a suit for alimony from his ex-wife. Kirkeby gives a court appearance by Waller's father as the reason for the pianist's relatively speedy release, but suggests that Anita Waller and the new baby were marooned in Chicago. This story is also recounted in Maurice Waller's biography of his father. There is nothing further to support this in the newspaper reports. The most significant mention of Fats in the Chicago press during May and June is an advertisement from the *Defender* of June 26 for Fats Waller, "internationally famed songwriter and Victor recording artist," endorsing "Washington Belle Hair Victory." This was one of a series of advertisements placed to "ballyhoo" Waller and Ellington by the same Harrison Smith who had been advertising manager of the Lincoln when Fats began playing there. "I arranged tie-ups of them . . . ballyhooing a hair tonic (which they never used) and got each 10,000 window posters for drugstores. Also full page ads in the *Defender* which cost $800 per page per issue . . . top brass at Victor were amazed by [this] overnight exploitation."[14]

In the fall of 1927, Fats made a break with the Lafayette, which was reported widely in the press. *The New York Age* of October 1 said: "Fats Waller, who has been playing the organ at the Lafayette Theater, was paid a visit by his wife one afternoon. She sat on the same stool with Fats while he was playing. The management objected. Words. Fats quit there and then." This seems a sharp contrast with the free and easy days at the Lincoln, but it shows something of the bond that had grown up between Fats and his second wife Anita that he quit his regular organ job for her.

The very end of 1927 found Fats preparing for a very important stage show. *Keep Shufflin'* was a vehicle for the comedians Miller and Lyles, who had been featured in Eubie Blake and Noble Sissle's highly successful show *Shuffle Along*. The new show was to have a book by the two principals and music, as both composers and performers, by the formidable team of James P. Johnson and Fats Waller. It marked a return for Fats to the kind of theater work he had undertaken as a performer with Katie Crippen, and as composer in the 1926 collaborations with Spencer Williams. Although he continued to work as a theater organist, the return from his season at the Vendome might be seen as a turning point towards the major part of his career in the musical theater.

Keep Shufflin' opened in Philadelphia at Gibson's Theater early in February 1928. After a two-week run there, it transferred to New York, where it opened on February 27 at Daly's Theater on Broadway and 63rd Street. The score had effectively been split down the middle, with about half the songs written by the team of Henry Creamer, Clarence Todd, and James P. Johnson, and the other half by Andy Razaf and Fats Waller. The hit song of the Philadelphia run was *Give Me the Sunshine* by Con Conrad, sung by the comedienne Jean Starr. Conrad was the producer of the show, although in reality it was backed by Arnold Rothstein, a gambler and underworld figure who had discovered that show business was an effective way to "launder" money from his less reputable pursuits.

The link between Conrad and the pupil–teacher team of Johnson and Waller was the almost ubiquitous figure in the world of Broadway music publishing, Perry Bradford. Bradford gives rather a good account of himself in his memoir *Born with the Blues* (published in 1965), but it was certainly gossip on the New York scene among African-American musicians that Bradford published many tunes that were not entirely his own work, and that many song pluggers would

demonstrate a new song to a music publisher only to find Bradford
stepping from a shady corner of the office and demanding a share of the
equity for transcribing the tune – or, worse still, claiming that he had
written the tune himself! In this case, however, he seems to have done
his fellow composers a favor by first suggesting Johnson, who in turn
recommended he share the job with Waller. Johnson was in the last
stages of composing his rhapsody for piano and orchestra *Yamekraw*,
and was also working on the music for a musical in collaboration with
Bradford, *Messin' Around*, which did not finally open until over a year
later, in April 1929, at the Hudson Theater. It is hardly surprising
therefore that he turned to Waller for help in composing the show for
Miller and Lyles. In addition, Waller and Johnson were to play together
in the pit band – teamed up at two pianos in a show-stopping
combination which proved so popular that they were featured every
night in the intermission, playing endless variations on Johnson's tune
from the show *'Sippi*.

The pit band for *Keep Shufflin'* was quite an array of talent, and
included the magnificent trumpeter Jabbo Smith and reedman Garvin
Bushell (of Liza's Shufflin' Sextet fame). Jabbo recalled the band with
affection in a conversation with the author in October 1986, and said it
had been a pleasure playing alongside "my buddy" Garvin Bushell. The
contemporary advertisements billed Jabbo "on the bugle," and in a
typical piece of hype referred to Fats and James P. in their piano duet as
"On the White Keys – Fats Waller! On the Black Keys – Jimmy
Johnson!"[15]

In fact, the pit band was led at first by Joe Jordan, rather than by
either of the show's composers. The *Chicago Defender* of February 25,
1928 announced: "Leads 'Keep Shufflin'' Music. Joe Jordan has been
chosen to direct the orchestra for Miller and Lyles' new show 'Keep
Shufflin'.' [The band includes] Jimmy Johnson, 'Fats' Waller and
Kenny, drummer. Johnson and Waller have several numbers in the
show." (Kenny was the erstwhile house drummer at Leroy's, Carl
"Battle Axe" Kenny.)

In many ways *Keep Shufflin'* took off because of its relationship to

The beaming pianist: three later studies of Waller at the keyboard.

the preceding show, *Shuffle Along.* The stars – Flourney Miller and Aubrey Lyles – were repeating the roles they had created for the earlier show, the characters Steve Jenkins and Sam Peck. The plot was the thinnest possible vehicle for a variety of good songs and dance routines, which, according to Gerald Bordman (the Broadway historian), was still the criterion by which the critics, and especially the white critics, judged a show.[16] The story involved the creation by the two protagonists of the "Equal Got League," which planned to blow up the local bank and redistribute the cash. In a fight to determine just which of the friendly society's members is man enough to be trusted with the job of the dynamiting, Steve Jenkins is knocked on the head. The second part of the show was a dream sequence in which the wealth and freedom for all that was the immediate consequence of the raid quickly gave way to anarchy and a breakdown of public order and services. Jenkins awakes from his dream in time to effect a turnaround of the plans and the re-establishment of the status quo.

What really mattered, of course, was the production and the strength of the songs and dance routines. Some papers thought the dancing went too far. The *World* talked of a chorus that danced with "ardor and ... grotesquerie," while on the other hand the *Herald-Tribune* thought the dancing not "negro" enough, and felt that the "beaming pianist" redeemed the evening. (This may, of course, have been either Waller or the equally beaming James P. Johnson.) Other reviews referred to the spectacular displays by "Battle Axe" the drummer.[17]

The musical arrangements for *Keep Shufflin'* had been prepared from the compositions of Waller and Johnson by Will Vodery (famous as the arranger for Ziegfeld's *Follies*), and these coupled with the intermission turn by the composers seem to have helped ensure the show's success on the musical front. Although Waller and Razaf's *Willow Tree* is well known as one of the hit songs from the show, it was not listed in the original program. Andy Razaf recalled: "The hit songs were *How Jazz Was Born* and *My Little Chocolate Bar.*"[18] Different accounts suggest that Johnson's *'Sippi* was also a hit. It is interesting to compare the list of songs from the first night of the show with a program from September the same year. In February, the show contained: *Charlie, My Back Door Man, Choc'late Bar, Dusky Love, Everybody's Happy in Jimtown, Exhortation, Give Me the Sunshine, Harlem Rose, How Jazz Was Born, Keep Shufflin', Labor Day Parade, Leg It, On the Levee, Opening Chorus, Pining, 'Sippi,* and *Washboard Ballet.*

By September, after seven months, it contained a very much realigned program: *Brothers, Bugle Blues, Choc'late Bar, Deep Blue Sea, Don't Wake 'Em Up, Give Me the Sunshine, Holiday in Jimtown, Keep Shufflin', Let's Go to Town, My Old Banjo, Pretty Soft, 'Sippi, Teasin' Baby, Where Jazz Was Born, Whoopem Up,* and *You May Be a Whale in Georgia.*

For the September program, *Willow Tree, Exhortation* (which was based on a theme from Johnson's rhapsody *Yamekraw*), *Got Myself Another Jockey Now, Skiddle de Skow,* and *'Twas a Kiss in the Moonlight* were listed as "additional numbers."

A month into the run, on March 27, 1928, a contingent from the show's pit band – Johnson, Waller, Bushell, and Jabbo Smith – went into the recording studio at Camden, New Jersey, to record two songs from the show, *'Sippi* and *Willow Tree,* as well as Rodger's *Thou Swell* (a tune beloved of stride pianists) and the Kahn–Moret number *Persian Rug.*

The idea of the recordings, or at least part of the idea, was to capture on wax the show-stopping duet of Waller and Johnson. But it didn't quite work out that way, since Waller (instead of being at a second piano, as he was in the show) was to play the organ, thus altering the tonal balance of the two keyboard parts entirely, and leading to a strange if charming set of sides. The best impression of the two-piano double act is not to be found on these sides at all, but on a piano roll of Johnson's, *If I Could Be with You,* which the two cut together for release in March 1927. In it, Waller's brilliant treble passages ornament James P.'s statement of the melody, and there is a

Jabbo Smith, photographed at the time of his starring role in the musical *One Mo' Time* in the early 1980s.

tremendous moment when they speed up together to go into the last chorus.

The recording problems of Camden are discussed in the next chapter. With regard to the March 1928 date itself, Garvin Bushell recalled:

> James P., I guess, had contracted with the Victor company. They wanted James P. and Fats on wax. So they took me and Jabbo – Jabbo was in the orchestra also. I remember the circumstances leading up to the date, and how it went over early in the morning, and a very early train to Philadelphia. We rehearsed over there. We'd been playing it, so we knew the tunes, so as far as getting it together, all we had to do was figure out how the routine was going to be. That's all we had to do.
>
> *Willow Tree* was in the show. It might have been a soft shoe number – it wasn't one of those slam-bang, knockout numbers. We were reading – I was reading music. And that was probably some of the first jazz bassoon was ever on Victor records. I

didn't play bassoon in the show, just alto and clarinet. But James P. had heard me playing the bassoon someplace – I think I played it in his *Yamekraw* – and he wanted me to do it, so I carried the bassoon with me to Camden. I got this baritone sax sound on the bassoon; that's why I could play jazz on it. It didn't sound like a bassoon. I used a different type of reed. I had used bassoon in Europe with Sam Wooding's orchestra, and there I was mainly playing from written out parts. I never took a bassoon solo with Sam. I was featured in some of the arrangements – *Covered Wagon*, and a couple of Indian melodies I used to play – but those records with James P. and Fats, that was the first time to my knowledge that anybody played jazz bassoon on records. There's a kind of an Adrian Rollini influence on that bassoon solo. He played bass sax. I was always fascinated with that.

Jabbo would do anything on trumpet, but we had a hard time keeping together with no drums, no bass. ... It took us a long time to get it that much together, loose as it was. See, I was a lead alto then. I wasn't really a jazzman. I wanted to play lead saxophone.

James P. was in charge of the date. He was conductor of the pit orchestra, so naturally he was the leader. Maybe Jimmy picked out the tunes from the show that he wanted to record. Victor must have picked out those two Broadway show tunes *Persian Rug* and *Thou Swell*.[19]

It seems to have been Victor, too, who chose the extraordinary name for the band, the Louisiana Sugar Babes. Garvin Bushell maintained, "I don't know who created the title. It had nothing whatsoever to do with the show." (Indeed, it wasn't until James P. and Fats were teamed up again on two pianos the following year, at a recording session with King Oliver's band under James P.'s leadership, that any attempt was made to cash in on the *Keep Shuffin'* name. The vocal trio on the Johnson–Waller–Oliver sides was called the "Keep Shufflin' Trio." The song they sang, *You've Got to Be Modernistic*, was not featured in *Keep Shufflin'*.)

Jabbo Smith talked to the author about the session, and remembered that Fats was "a beautiful guy, full of fun, both on and off the stage." He "went on tour with the pit band of *Keep Shufflin'*, but when the show folded in Chicago, I stayed. Chicago was fabulous! I found a job right off at the Sunset Café."[20] Jabbo was a virtuoso trumpeter, considered by many as almost equal in ability to Armstrong during the late 1920s. His presence in the show must have led to some brilliant musical moments, and it may be on his account that *Bugle Blues* was introduced into the program. The end of the tour came in Chicago, when Rothstein, its backer, was murdered in November 1928. Fats had, in fact, already left the show, having gone to Philadelphia in June to take up a short-term job as organist at the Royal Grand Theater.

Before Fats's departure, another significant event occurred. On April 27 he gave the première of Johnson's rhapsody *Yamekraw* at Carnegie Hall. By all accounts, Johnson had intended to play the piano himself on this auspicious occasion. The work was given at a recital jointly arranged by the "Father of the Blues," W. C. Handy, and the poet Robert Clairmont. Despite being described by Handy as "a hatless bohemian from the 'Village,'" Clairmont had put up $5000 of his own money to help Handy present what was grandiosely described as "a concert to show the evolution of Black music." A chorus of 60 and a 30-piece orchestra performed works by Handy, Joplin, J. Rosamond Johnson, James A. Bland, and – finally – James P. Johnson.[21]

Both Ed Kirkeby and Johnson's biographer Scott Brown make it clear that Miller and Lyles would not release Johnson from *Keep Shufflin'* to play at America's leading concert hall in the première of his first major extended composition for piano and orchestra. But little explanation is proffered.

In fact, two things conspired to make Fats Waller the expendable part of the keyboard duo for the evening. The first (as we know from Garvin Bushell's account) is that, by the end of March, Johnson had taken over leadership of the pit band from Joe Jordan. Obviously the second pianist was less important to the show than the bandleader. The second fact is that on April 23 the show had transferred from Daly's "out-of-the-way" house (as Bordman called it) to the downtown Eltinge Theater on 42nd Street, West of Broadway. Obviously, Miller and Lyles were not going to prejudice the smooth running of the transfer by releasing the bandleader for the night only four days after the move, let alone by allowing him the necessary rehearsal time when he was no doubt required to break in the cast of the show in their new home.

The Carnegie Hall debut was very good for the young Waller's career, and he so impressed Handy and Clairmont in his audition that he was asked to include a selection of his own organ solos in the program as well as performing *Yamekraw*.

After leaving *Keep Shufflin'*, and following the Philadelphia engagement, Waller began work on another musical, this time to be written entirely by himself and Andy Razaf, entitled *Load of Coal*. Once more the chronology is confused, but Kirkeby gives early 1929 for the date of composition. However, Fats was imprisoned for a period beginning in August 1928 until December 1928. Both Kirkeby and Maurice Waller's accounts suggest that Fats was bailed out by Gene Austin, and it was possibly during this period of bail that Fats attended the birth of his third son Ronald on October 26, 1928. But neither the comprehensive *Storyville* discography of Waller, nor Paul Machlin's supplementary 1985 recording chronology gives any hint of the recording session that is alleged to have been Austin's excuse for springing Fats.

T. Magnusson, in an article in the *Journal of Jazz Studies*, puts up a convincing case that the pianist on Austin's November 1928 sessions is not Waller. (Fats did take part in a recording with Austin in June 1929 but this latter date is too late to have any relevance to the bail controversy.[22]) Waller began work on his next show, *Hot Chocolates*, in April 1929 or thereabouts, since it opened in May. The *Load of Coal* collaboration, therefore, may possibly have been before the spell in prison, rather than after (as Kirkeby suggests), or it may date from the time of Fats's release.[23] Waller's activities are unclear from the time he was out of prison for good until his recording session on March 1, 1929 with his "Buddies."

The prison sentence was a consequence of what Fats's son Maurice referred to as his father's selective memory. The pianist simply forgot to continue the alimony payments to his former wife. *Variety* reported in its issue of September 19, 1928:

> Fats Waller sent away; abandoned family. Fats Waller has been sentenced to serve from six months to three years in the New York County Jail, charged with the abandonment of his wife Edith Waller and their four year old son Thomas Jr.
>
> When Fats was hailed before Judge Albert Cohn in the Bronx County Court he was wistful and repentant. He told the judge he had been in jail thirty one days and had learned his lesson. [This implies that he had actually been incarcerated from mid-August.] The judge told Fats he had had five lessons already.
>
> Sometime ago, Mrs. Waller was awarded $20 weekly alimony, but Waller slipped up on the payments.

Whichever side of the prison sentence Fats actually worked on *Load of Coal*, it was almost certainly the first floorshow that he composed for the nightclub Connie's Inn.

Fats was a familiar figure at Connie's, the nightclub next door to the Lafayette Theater, run by Connie and George Immerman, who had employed the teenage Fats as a delivery boy for their delicatessen. Fats worked at the club as a pianist, both as soloist and from time to time with the house band. The trombonist Dicky Wells played briefly with Fats in the house band at Connie's.

"We were supposed to finish at 4 o'clock," he told Stanley Dance, "but Fats would put his derby on the piano after the second show and tell us to go home. They'd fill his derby up with money and he'd be singing or composing songs, and we'd be on the street, or down the Hoofer's club."[24]

The arrangements at Connie's Inn were roughly the same as those at the rival cabaret, Smalls' Paradise. We can get a good idea of a musician's life at Smalls' from the autobiography of Benny Waters, who worked there with Charlie Johnson's orchestra. Both clubs mounted full staged revues of the kind that *Load of Coal* was no doubt intended to be.

"They changed the show every three months or so. We had to rehearse all the music as we kept getting new people. The chorus girls remained there all the time. It was the stars who changed."[25]

Benny was at Smalls' during the latter part of the 1920s through into 1930, when he played in James P. Johnson's musical *Kitchen Mechanics Revue*. This was one of Johnson's best shows, and contained several of his hit songs, including *A Porter's Love Song*, which Fats was later to record as one of the earliest tracks with his recording group, the Rhythm. "The show lasted two hours at least and we were on twice a night. In between the show we played for dancing and sometimes people came in at closing time and payed us extra money to play the show again."[26]

A cabaret band such as Charlie Johnson's did not restrict itself to the club in which it was based – often playing at Harlem theaters, for one-off dance engagements, and making records. Waters recalled:

I will never forget one particular day when we did three things. Early in the morning we went down to Camden. We recorded all day, and by the time we came back and ate it was time to go to Smalls'. Then after that, at 4am, we had to go and play a breakfast dance that lasted until nine in the morning.

When the band had an early evening theater job it would simply engage a substitute orchestra for the first show at Smalls'. From all accounts, very much the same went on at Connie's Inn. There was an equivalent turnover of personnel in the bands there, and no doubt the music was constantly being rehearsed for new members of the group. When Dicky Wells was in the band, it also included the star trumpeters

Red Allen and Frankie Newton, as well as the great drummer Big Sid Catlett. Wells remembered: "One night Frank was playing a solo, and Fats started to stride and overshadow him. So Frank stopped playing and asked Fats how much he wanted to cool it. Fats smiled and said 'Half a buck.' Frank gave it to him and started blowing again, no hard feelings."[27]

Wells recalled that the chorus line at Connie's Inn was made up of girls and drag artists, who were so good that paying customers could seldom tell the difference. Acts that worked in the club during Wells's stay included the Mills Brothers, Snake Hips Tucker, and a "shake dancer," Louise Cook. Other names were Bill Bailey, Jackie Mabley, and Paul Myers. Wells recollected that from time to time the entire show from a cabaret would be booked into one of the theaters, such as the Lafayette, "because people couldn't afford all those stiff cabaret prices." There was an accepted practice that the theaters would feature a different band every week, which usually worked up on the stage both as a featured act and to accompany the show.

The choreographer at the Inn was Leonard Harper, who had worked with Fats in the 1926 shows at the Lafayette. There are two good memoirs of Fats at work on rehearsing a show with Harper, the first from the pianist and composer Mary Lou Williams (telling her life story to Max Jones for the *Melody Maker* in 1954) and the second from the clarinetist and Harlem character Milton "Mezz" Mezzrow (talking to Madeleine Gautier for the *Bulletin* of the Hot Club of France).

Mary Lou recalled Waller sitting "overflowing the piano stool" with his jug of whisky nearby. Harper called out to ask what Fats had written for the next routine, and – according to Mary Lou – Fats made up the show there and then, improvising something appropriate for each routine. (She goes on to say that she was then offered a bet by a fellow musician that she couldn't repeat from memory everything she had just heard Fats play. Fats took up the bet, roaring with delight as she succeeded in reproducing virtually everything.)

"Not long afterwards, Harper asked me how I'd like to work at

Mary Lou Williams talking to Charlie Shavers: Paris 1954. This was the date of her long interview with Max Jones concerning Fats Waller.

Connie's Inn. I would, and I began playing the intermission piano while the band was over at the Lafayette Theater, just up the Avenue, by the Tree of Hope, where musicians used to exchange stories and await work."[28]

Despite Mary Lou's personal involvement as intermission pianist at the Inn, her account doesn't quite tally with the other reports of Fats at work on a show. There is no doubt he was a brilliant inventor of catchy tunes and could come up almost at will with appropriate melodies for the lyrics of Razaf, J. C. Johnson, and the other writers with whom he worked. But his background in the theater and his involvement in writing other shows suggest he was far more the conventional professional show composer than Mary Lou would like us to think. She was, after all, recalling events of twenty-five years before when talking to Max Jones, and probably felt justified in enhancing the reputation of a man she obviously greatly admired. We know that he worked hard on rehearsing the routines – something that would be virtually impossible with improvised tunes of uncertain structure. Also, brilliant writer that Fats was, we know he could seldom remember what he had composed unless it was committed quickly to paper. If we treat Mary Lou's account with a certain amount of artistic license, we can then conclude that Fats was pretty mercurial about the manner in which he and Razaf actually worked: he frequently left Razaf to commit their ideas to paper, but once the material had been written the team worked hard with their producer in getting the routines into shape.

Mezz recalled Fats sitting at the piano at Connie's Inn (which he described as a "cellar" – not a "cave" as mistranslated in *Hear Me Talkin' to Ya*) with his hat off and his collar open, constantly reworking a theme with new embellishments until it was right. Razaf would be in a corner polishing up the lyrics, and coming over to the piano from time to time to try out the new versions. He sang well, and Mezz thought the team should appear together in the show, but Fats, at this stage in his career, was emphatic that he was a musician, not an actor.

Mezz Mezzrow (left) with Sidney Bechet at one of the mid-1940s *King Jazz* sessions.

(Razaf later recorded as a singer – notably the following year with Luis Russell.) The main thing that Mezz remembered about the atmosphere was the hum of activity, "vibrant with laughter, gaiety, and enthusiasm." But above all, his account smacks of hard work: of polishing, refining, and rehearsing – but not composing from scratch at the keyboard. Such a thing would also be unlikely with Harper running the show. He was "one of the most formidable producers of revues who I've ever met," recalled Mezz.

> He was a black producer who, if he hadn't died young, and if by some miracle he'd had the chance, could have made most of the Hollywood dance numbers of later days seem stupid and lightweight. He ran through the rehearsal with the dancers on the floor, showing them the routines, guiding each number.[29]

The difficulty in writing a show with Fats, according to Andy Razaf, was pinning him down in one place long enough to do the work in advance.

> My mother used to make all the finest food and special cookies for him at our home in Asbury Park, N.J. We were working on a show called *Load of Coal* for Connie, and had just done half the chorus of a number when Fats remembered a date and announced "I gotta go." I finished up the verse and gave it to him later over the telephone. The tune was *Honeysuckle Rose*.
>
> ... Fats was the most prolific and the fastest writer I ever knew. He could set a melody to any lyric, and he took great pains working on it, getting the exact mood and phrasing until the melody would just pour from his fingers. I used to say he could set the telephone book to music. He took great pride in doing an accurate perfect job, with every note in the right place, so much so that even if he finished a whole piano copy in half an hour, it could be sent right down to the printers without any changes.[30]

This is hardly a picture of a man who composed shows as he went along.

From earlier biographies of Waller, we can infer that *Load of Coal* contained three of the best-known tunes by Razaf and Waller. These were *Honeysuckle Rose, Zonky,* and *My Fate Is in Your Hands.* Contemporary accounts suggest that *Honeysuckle Rose* was not prominently featured in the show. But it is hardly fair to suggest (as do Ed Kirkeby and Maurice Waller) that it was thereby relegated to obscurity until a film was made some fifteen years later suggesting that Waller had composed it in prison (to the great annoyance of Razaf, who conducted a hotly defensive correspondence with *Variety* on the issue). The tune immediately became the anthem of the New York jam session, and has remained so ever since. *Honeysuckle Rose* was so much the natural vehicle for swing bands that it formed a major part of Benny Goodman's famous January 1938 Carnegie Hall concert, where it was the automatic choice for a freewheeling performance that united players from the bands of Goodman, Basie, and Ellington.

Waller and Razaf's next collaboration was the high point of Fats's theater career and provided one of those rare moments in Broadway history when a host of diffuse elements came together and created a show that truly filled the potential of the sum of its parts. *Hot Chocolates* confirmed Waller as one of the finest composers of popular songs, gave a considerable fillip to the career of Cab Calloway, and was perhaps the single most important element in transforming Louis Armstrong from a magnificent jazz musician into a star of the popular entertainment world. The two most enduring songs that Fats wrote for this show were *Ain't Misbehavin'* and *Black and Blue.* The first has a catchy melody, with the usual 32-bar structure of the jazz standard, but with a middle section or "channel" that builds climactically into the reprise of the first theme, avoiding the usual paraphrase of *I Got Rhythm.* The second, in a unique blend of lyric and theme, became a noble statement of the predicament of African-American people in America. It was taken up gradually as the song that, before Billie

Holiday's *Strange Fruit*, expressed the plight of a people, each of whom could identify with the line "My only sin is my skin."

Hot Chocolates opened at Connie's Inn in May 1929. It quickly proved so successful that the Immermans decided to move it to a theater. The *New York Age* tells us on June 1 that the show was to transfer under the headline "Hot Chocolates from Connie's to open Windsor Theater, Bronx." It went on, "For half a dozen years, Connie's has housed the colored show par excellence. In those years Connie has gathered together Negro artists of the first water," and detailed the names of the stars of the new show, among whom were James Baskette (who later came to fame as Uncle Remus in Disney's *Song of the South*) and Eddie Green.

After the Bronx tryout it was intended that the show should transfer to Broadway itself, a move that should have taken place during the week of June 15, but the *Age* reported: "*Hot Chocolate* [sic] did not open at the Hudson Theater this week as planned. Several changes had to be made before they will open."

The show finally went on at the Hudson on June 20. It was to run for 219 performances, and during much of that run the cast returned to Connie's after each performance to repeat the program at the club. In *Ain't Misbehavin'* Ed Kirkeby reproduces many of the reviews from the press, and they are universal in their praise for "the best Negro revue since Blackbirds." Most of them mention the dancer Jazz Lips Richardson and his colleague Baby Cox. The other item singled out for praise was the song *Ain't Misbehavin'*, and it is in the *New York Times* review that the final part of the success story is first noted: "One song, an entirely pleasant jazz ballad called 'Ain't Misbehavin'' stands out, and its rendition between the acts by an unnamed member of the orchestra was a highlight of the premiere."[31]

Armstrong's part in the show was steadily increased. Mezz Mezzrow recalled the rehearsals.

> Imagine, in a corner of the club, Louis Armstrong blowing his
> trumpet, accompanied by Fats at the piano, both trying to get

the most out of the piece they were playing ... the thing that dominated the show above all else was Louis and Fats. To see these two geniuses at work, two of the most magnetic and attractive personalities in the world, was something that will remain deeply engraved in my memory. Louis would start by playing the tunes in the lower register of the trumpet, with a tone as big as Fats himself. I have never heard the equal of those low, round, full notes which came from the instrument. No other trumpeter could produce them, and believe me, I've heard plenty of trumpeters!

Mezz goes on to describe the earliest rehearsals of *Ain't Misbehavin'*, at which Fats sang the song through for Louis, while the latter made up an accompaniment on the trumpet that was "the most pure and authentic blues."[32]

Waller in his dressing room.

Press advertisements for the show were lively. Fats, the by now rather rotund Louis, and the singer Edith Wilson were described as "1,000 lbs of rhythm." The Hudson Theater panel in the *New York Age* billed "Leroy Smith's Orchestra and Connie's Sun-tanned Beauty Chorus."

Armstrong himself spent the last week of June playing an early evening show at the Lafayette Theater as well as *Hot Chocolates* at the Hudson and Connie's, and his group (the former Carroll Dickerson Orchestra from Chicago) took over from Leroy Smith as the house band at Connie's while Smith was leading the music for the Hudson Theater. There is no doubt that this spell in New York was a vital turning point in Armstrong's career, but at the same time it is obvious that Louis owed his popular success to sheer hard work at a level daunting for most of his sidemen, let alone with the added pressure of having to perform on stage as singer and soloist and live up to the reputation claimed for him in his contemporary press advertisements as the "World's Greatest Cornetist."

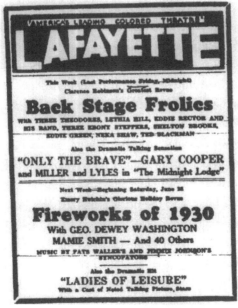

Amsterdam News advertisement for *Fireworks of 1930.*

While Louis was building his career on the back of the show, Fats managed one of the biggest misjudgments of his career: on July 17, 1929 he sold the copyrights in virtually all the hit songs from *Hot Chocolates* and several more of his compositions to Irving Mills for the reported sum of $500. Kirkeby gives Waller the benefit of the doubt that this may have been the advance on a series of stage payments, but if Waller's track record is anything to go by, then he probably did sign away the title to such hits as *Ain't Misbehavin'*, *Black and Blue*, and *Sweet Savannah Sue*. Had he sold them in a more commercial manner, the royalties from these might well have prevented Fats from falling into many of the problems over alimony and maintenance that bedeviled much of his life. At least in August of that year, when he made one of his finest collections of recorded piano solos (featuring many of the tunes he had sold), he recouped some further income from his work.[33]

Hot Chocolates ran on into the spring of 1930, and it enjoyed several revivals. (A notable one in 1932 featured Armstrong once more.) In the latter part of 1929, Fats took part in a large number of recording sessions; he also continued to compose, another notable hit from the period being *I've Got a Feeling I'm Falling*. He had begun to appear on stage as a solo artist, and in February 1930 the newspapers announced that he would be taking up a solo residency at Connie's Inn, "where an organ has been installed for the special performances to be given by Mr. Waller."[34]

In April 1930, Werba's Brooklyn Theater mounted a show loosely based on one of Fats's earlier theater pieces and entitled *Shuffle Along of 1930*. It passed off its principal actors as being Miller and Lyles, but in fact this was a hoax, and the press criticized the show widely. But if this Johnson and Waller revival was not a success, it wasn't long before the team produced another collaborative musical revue. This time it was for the Lafayette Theater, and opened on Saturday June 28 as a "Fourth of July Special" under the title *Fireworks of 1930*. Fats Waller and Jimmie Johnson's Syncopators were billed as the orchestra, and the stars included Mamie Smith. It ran for a single week.

The year 1930 was the final one of Fats's creative output for the stage until thirteen years later, shortly before his death, when he worked with George Marion Jr. on the show *Early to Bed*. But before jumping forward to look at that musical, it is important to realize just how far Fats had come since his debut as organist at the Lincoln, and his early efforts with Liza and Her Shufflin' Sextet, seven years before.

The easiest way to examine Fats's reputation in 1930 is to look at his billing from the theaters that advertised his appearances. His August 1930 visit to Chicago is an ideal opportunity, and we find the Regal Theater using a very different description from that used only a year or two earlier by the Vendome:

Extra added attraction – the one and only
FATS WALLER
Composer of *Ain't Misbehavin'*, *Black and Blue*
and 400 Hits!

It is easy to see from this how the emphasis had changed. Fats was no longer the "sensational organist," but the established composer of nationally known hit songs, who was a stage personality in his own right. Along with Sammy Dyer and the Regalettes, the Regal's advertisements for August 16 billed "FATTS WALLER" [*sic*] as one of "two charming stage shows."[35] In the next chapter, Fats's transition from stage and club performer to radio star will be discussed, but before leaving his work in the theater we should move on to 1943 and *Early to Bed*.

In many ways, this show epitomizes the triumph and the tragedy of Waller's life. By the early 1940s, he had become a national celebrity, and the show was planned as a vehicle for him by the producer Dick Kollmar. However, when Fats was signed up as the star, although George Marion had written the book and lyrics, no composer had been found for the score. Ed Kirkeby talked Kollmar into commissioning the music from Waller, and this is what happened.

By the time the show actually opened, Waller had withdrawn from the cast, despite having written the score well on time. (He apparently rang the producer while in his cups and offered to sell the whole copyright outright for some instant cash – an alarming repeat of his behavior with Irving Mills over the hits from *Hot Chocolates*. Kollmar was so alarmed by this that he pressed Kirkeby into guaranteeing that Waller would finish off the couple of songs remaining at the time and withdraw from the cast.) The show ran to packed houses in Boston and New York, and Waller's name was up in lights, but the show's opening in Boston, which should have been the high point of Fats's life – a triumphal return to the musical stage with the hit songs *Slightly Less Than Wonderful* and *This Is So Nice It Must Be Illegal* – was marred by one of the worst and most blatant examples of racial discrimination of his whole career. It is a commentary on the different status of Waller in the 1940s from his role in the 1920s that the new show was opening in a white theater district in New England, while his earlier hits had been based in the African-American clubland and theaters of Harlem. It is unlikely that discrimination would have been a problem for Fats during the runs at Connie's Inn (although most of the patrons were white), but despite his status as a national celebrity he ran up against it in Boston in the 1940s.

There is a summary of the incident in Ed Kirkeby's biography. As Fats's manager, Kirkeby had wired ahead to their hotel and made advance bookings for himself, Fats, and Anita. "The clerk, seeing Fats and Anita standing in the lobby and observing their color coldly disclaimed having any such reservations."[36] The show opened as planned on May 24, 1943 at the Shubert Theater, but after the parties, the receptions, and the bouquets, the composer returned to what his friend the saxophonist and singer Joey Nash described as a "flop joint."

Nash had first encountered Fats during the mid-1920s on a train from Washington to New York, and met him again during the first run of *Hot Chocolates*; Fats had made contact with him for the opening of *Early to Bed*, since Nash was working at one of the smart Boston hotels. Fats invited Nash to the Shubert Theater early on the morning of his arrival, and together they found a bar near the theater where Fats played over the songs from the show. This was an old ritual of pleasure for the two. Fats used to do the round of the Broadway music publishers with Nash and play over songs that one or the other might feature in their respective radio shows. Nash recalled,

> He was excited about every song, stopping to repeat, again and again, phrases and chords he particularly fancied. Waller's artistry made it a day never to be recaptured: the back room of a saloon became a concert hall, a two hour recital for a mesmerized audience of one. Waller's touch gave the scarred upright the sonority and bell-like tone of a concert grand, filling the room with etudes of ecstasy, sentimental songs and rocking riffs. *Early to Bed* was a triumph for Fats, every song was a gem.

Later that day, expecting Fats to be caught up in the promotional round of events organized around the première by the show's backers, Nash was surprised to be telephoned by Fats, who asked him to come straight over.

> His dismal room was the size of an iron lung. Overhead, banging steam pipes hammered out a morse code rhythm. A drab, patched bedspread and a rust stained wash basin hit my eyes.
>
> "Can I do anything?" I asked.
>
> "Yes. That's why I called you," he answered. "You've been working and living at your hotel for some weeks, so, by now, you must know the manager, the assistant manager, or the head reservations clerk. I want a suite. I want the best. Get on the telephone won't you?"
>
> I went downstairs and called. I knew the top brass in the 750 room hotel. They all liked me. The assistant manager gave me a friendly greeting and listened to my request. Sorry – but he just couldn't help me or Fats Waller. It would cost him his job. I had a room on the tenth floor, all to myself with twin

beds. Couldn't I share my room with Fats? The assistant manager's voice now verged on the hysterical. He shouted that if I tried "that trick" he'd throw me and Waller out of the hotel.[37]

Nash was powerless to do anything to help, and Fats left immediately to return to New York, where he had canceled a lucrative nightclub engagement to attend the opening of his show in Boston. According to Maurice Waller, Fats filled in during the extension of the show's Boston run by taking a week's booking in Philadelphia. Eventually, the play followed Fats to New York and opened at the Broadhurst Theater on Thursday June 17, 1943. The retreat from Boston was one of the worst examples of prejudice to affect Fats.

Herman Autrey, the trumpeter in Fats's 1930s small band, said that Fats was more acutely aware of prejudice than his outward

Waller embarking on a much more successful attempt at air travel than that described by Herman Autrey (publicity photo for United Airlines).

appearance might have led people to believe. For an African-American musician in the USA it was an ever present threat.

> At that time a Negro couldn't just walk in anywhere and buy a sandwich, not even to go. . . . There was a time in California, I guess in 1935 or 1936, we'd played some theaters, and when the tour was over he'd made arrangements to hurry home to his family in New York. The manager made the booking for him with the airline. His name was actually Thomas Wright Waller, and when he arrived at the airport he told them his name. "We thought you were white" they said. "Well, I'm coloured, so what?" Fats said. Anyway they said he couldn't go on the plane. He went home by train. And the plane he was booked on crashed in Kansas City, which is where he died [seven years later] in 1943.[38]

All African-American musicians could recount similar stories. Danny Barker, in an interview with the author, said that he thought the worst aspect in many ways was the sheer difficulty of traveling about in some parts of the country:

> It was a thing with all black show people having emergencies and hitting the bushes on the highways and byways, because the segregation laws did not allow black backsides to sit on the same toilet seats as white backsides. . . . All coloured performers knew this situation, as they were born with the laws, so hitting the bushes was generally something of a laugh.[39]

Safe from the problems of Boston, Fats saw *Early to Bed* open in New York to a mixed but satisfactory press. It continued to run throughout the season. Joel Vance, in his life of Fats, speculates that the show (which was very much in the old-fashioned mode of Broadway show, and had little original material to offer) would not have done so well without the wartime need for entertainment. Certainly it was this need that led to Fats's recordings of three of his

> "*The most beautiful chorus in the land*"
> Nichols, Times
>
> Richard Kollmar's *Musical Comedy Hit*
>
> # EARLY TO BED
>
> Muriel   Mary   Leonard   Bob
> ANGELUS   SMALL   CEELEY   HOWARD
>
> *Book and Lyrics by* GEORGE MARION JR.
>
> *Music by* THOMAS ("FATS") WALLER
>
>
>
> BROADHURST   W. 44 St., CI. 6-6699

Press advertisement for
the New York run of
Early to Bed.

songs from the show for V-disc, on September 16, 1943. Evidently
somewhat the worse for drink, Fats lost no opportunity to emphasize
the connection between *Slightly Less Than Wonderful, There's a Girl in
My Life,* and *This Is So Nice It Must Be Illegal* and his hit show on
Broadway. (He plugged the show again on a WABC *Off the Record*
interview with Hugh Conover, a week later, on September 23, when he
played an excellent version of *There's a Girl in My Life,* a recording of
which survives.)

In the V-disc session (made in the Victor studios) there is an
extraordinary contrast between the delicacy and finesse with which the
pianist's hands negotiate the keyboard, from time to time playing
stunning runs or delicate ornaments on the themes, and the slurred
coarseness of his speech as he shouts: "Hello boys, I'm goin' to give you
a couple of tunes from my show *Early to Bed,* a fine show on Broadway
that pays my back house dues, you know. I can't kid no more, but here's
a couple of them from the show."

In the middle of *There's a Girl in My Life* he suddenly calls out, "Oh what a half pint would do right now," and in the vocal, between shouting out asides that are far from his usual funny quips, he has a relaxation in the placing of the words that is not quite controlled. The introduction to *This Is So Nice* suffers the same way and the vocal itself is slurred. Yet Waller's playing on the first act closing number, *Martinique*, is his usual clear piano work over a Latin rhythm, despite his carrying on a conversation with someone else in the studio whose asides are vaguely audible, and who prompts him into some rather un-funny cod Spanish. It is not until *Motherless Child*, the last of a set of organ solos from the same session, that Fats's fingers falter in a manner approaching that of his vocals. It is sad that this, which is almost his last recorded work, suffers from a slightly less than wonderful performance.

Early to Bed had a rather thin plot set in a Martinique bordello, the Angry Pigeon, in which a bullfighter, El Magnifico, and his son arrive at the same time as a track team that hopes to use the place as a training headquarters. Neither party seems to notice the real business carried on there, and matters are further complicated by the fact that the madame, Rowena, is a former schoolteacher, who is recognized as such by the bullfighter.

It marks Fats's final association with the Broadway stage. In contrast with James P. Johnson, Fats had taken other directions during the 1930s, notably into radio and bandleading. Johnson, although developing his interest in symphonic composition, remained to some extent involved in the theater, and was left behind by his former protégé. Throughout the 1930s, Johnson continued the pattern that he and Fats had set in the 1920s – shows for Connie, the Lafayette, and a variety of other New York theaters. Johnson even essayed an opera in collaboration with Langston Hughes, the poet and writer central to the so-called Harlem Renaissance, and *The Organizer* was given at Carnegie Hall during 1940. Nevertheless, by the 1930s, Johnson no longer thought that the theater carried the same possible rewards as other forms of entertainment, even if it offered a more controllable workload. He felt out on something of a limb:

I had just come out of the period when I was in show business. I looked down on dance bands. In a dance band you had to work all night. I was making big money and dance bands weren't making big money. Then in Chicago Paul Ash introduced a new form of entertainment – the band on the stage. Well, they began to sell bands for a lot of money after that. I was misplaced. I didn't have an orchestra.[40]

The end of Fats's main theater career in 1930 marked the point of his change of direction. In a way, as for Louis Armstrong, it was *Hot Chocolates* that had opened the doors for other avenues of Waller's career. In his case, however, it was not immediate fame as a singer and entertainer that he found, but the acclaim that goes with having written a string of hits. With the onset of the Depression, while Johnson dug in and prepared *Kitchen Mechanics*, *Sugar Hill*, *Harlem Hotcha*, and a number of other shows, Fats looked to his talents as a solo nightclub artist, and to radio, for the next stage of his career.

James P. Johnson: a publicity shot for his revue *Sugar Hill* in its 1949 revival.

THE RHYTHM AND
THE BIG BAND

An increasingly important aspect of Fats Waller's work during the late 1920s was his freelance recording career, which he maintained in addition to his own contract with Victor as an organ and piano soloist. But in 1929, in the wake of the Wall Street crash and the ensuing Depression, there were dramatic changes in the American recording industry. From the advent of electrical recording in 1925, it had reached its zenith in 1927 with an output of just under 100 million discs. This level was maintained until 1929. By 1932, record sales had leveled off at the post-Depression plateau; a figure of just six million a year.

Earlier biographers of Waller have pondered on the cutback in his recording career between 1929 and 1934. Between January 1930 and May 1934, Waller took part in just six studio recording sessions, compared with fifteen during 1929 alone. Against the background of as severe a recession as the figures above demonstrate, he might be considered lucky to have maintained a foothold in the industry at all. The six sessions were all in their way significant; from the first with Ted Lewis (in which Fats's singing as a soloist was first recorded) to the musical high points of that with Billy Banks's Rhythmakers in 1932, they were all memorable.

Far more importantly than his career on record, Fats's attention was turned to developing his skills as a radio performer, something he had begun in the early 1920s but until the time of the crash had pursued only half-heartedly. As he turned his back (for the time being) on the theater, he moved further into broadcasting.

For part of the period 1929 to 1934, Fats's club work continued. He worked either as a solo act, or, for example, in Otto Hardwicke's band at the Hotfeet Club, 142 West Houston Street, in Greenwich Village. But in one sense this was simply a continuation of what he had been doing for some years.

A major change was that Waller obtained a proper manager, Phil Ponce, who improved the business side of his career and steered him towards becoming a popular radio artist. From December 1930 until June 1931, Fats appeared on "Paramount on Parade." In 1931 he was on "Radio Roundup," and in 1932, after his visit to Paris (discussed in Chapter 5), he moved to Cincinnati, Ohio, where radio station WLW gave him his own program, "Fats Waller's Rhythm Club," as well as a late-night show, "Moon River," on which he performed anonymously, playing standard tunes on the organ. Although "Moon River" was popular with the non jazz-minded public, it was the "Rhythm Club" that made Fats's reputation with the Midwest radio audience. To some extent, it involved adapting his nightclub technique for the microphone. At the Hotfeet Club, Fats had held his own as a cabaret turn amid singing waiters and the full band sets. He began satirizing the lyrics of his songs and punctuating them with risqué patter. (His subsequent manager Ed Kirkeby recalls some of these gags in his book *Ain't Misbehavin'*, such as, "A cow accidentally ate a bee, and the bee got so mad it swore to sting the cow in its stomach. However, on the way down it fell asleep; and when it woke up, the cow had gone.")[1] On the Cincinnati show, "Fats Waller's Rhythm Club," a format was adopted that allowed Fats to develop this approach.

Appearing with the announcer Paul Stewart and a singing group called the Southern Suns, Fats effected weekly the conversion of a stern deacon from warning sinners against the devil's music into a state in which the deacon himself began to enjoy the music of Fats, the Southern Suns, and the house band, Eddie Johnson's St Louis Crackerjacks, which included several future stars such as trumpeter Harry "Sweets" Edison and altoist "Tab" Smith. The show ran for a year. During the period in Cincinnati, Fats borrowed Johnson's band for weekend gigs, which, according to drummer Lester "Spare Rib" Nichols (who played on these jobs), were spread over the "territories" of Ohio, Kentucky, and Indiana. "On Monday he'd have to be back in Cincinnati for the broadcasts. ... We'd start to play, Fats would sing two or three choruses and have the tenor or trumpet take one, and then he could be heard hollering over the ensemble."[2]

When he returned to New York, Waller achieved a considerable reputation as a consequence of yet another series of radio performances that went out from March to June 1934, culminating in a twice-weekly version of the "Rhythm Club."

It was during this period from the Wall Street crash to the revival of his own studio career in 1934, that Fats was recorded as a singer, with Ted Lewis (March 1931), and Paul Machlin advances the theory that it was Waller's exposure on radio that developed his verbal and singing skills. On live radio, he points out, "it was necessary to retain almost constant verbal contact with the audience, sometimes at the expense of the music itself."[3] We know from recordings that have survived of Waller's many radio broadcasts that he developed his own trademarks. Some of them, such as the repeated "Hallo! Hallo!," were Harlem jive talk, and musicians of Waller's generation occasionally introduce such jive into their conversation even today. Exaggerated English accents were another typical piece of jive. On many of Fats's recordings he sings the long English "can't" rather than the American version with its shortened vowel sound, and jokes abounded about "cups of tea" and "old chaps."

A recording such as the 1938 *You Look Good to Me* has a commentary over the later solos that captures much of the spirit of this banter. So when the Victor company offered Waller a recording contract in 1934, it was evident that this was planned to capitalize on

Eddie Condon, who recalled his recording session with Fats in the book *We Called It Music*.

Waller's reputation for quick-witted humor and vocals, every bit as much as for his skills as pianist, composer, and bandleader. Radio had the power to make the reputation of performers in a way that no other medium could. It was radio, for instance, that was credited for the extraordinary success of the Benny Goodman Orchestra in the mid-1930s. The band's reputation was made on the West Coast by an East Coast radio show which, although it went out late in the evening in New York, was broadcast in the West at prime time on account of the time difference.

Characteristically, Waller seems to have been somewhat haphazard about assembling the band that became known as "Fats Waller and his Rhythm." Eddie Condon recounted in his autobiography the casual way in which the March 1, 1929 session by "Fats Waller and his Buddies" came to be made. On that occasion Fats entrusted the assembly of the sidemen to a few last minute telephone calls that followed a riotous tour of nightspots with Condon. Not all that much had changed by 1934.

At the start of his new Victor contract, Fats was very active on radio, but still making frequent club appearances. After a spell at the uptown Pod's and Jerry's (where Billie Holiday had made her debut), Fats opened at Adrian's Tap Room in the basement of the downtown President Hotel. The club was run by the multi-instrumentalist Adrian Rollini. Ed Kirkeby gives a rather grandiose description of it in *Ain't Misbehavin'*, talking of a talented group of waiters who would switch from table service to dancing at a moment's notice. Danny Barker, who worked there the following year (1935), told the author: "Adrian had one bartender, two waiters, and a Chinese in the back cooking the food." According to him, the club was "a little niche on the right side of the hotel."[4] The great thing, though, about the Tap Room was that it was beneath the President, which was a musicians' hotel. Principally the Tap Room was a haunt of the white big bands, but the clientele of the hotel upstairs assured Fats of a steady stream of enthusiastic musicians in the audience and as sitters-in. (The bands that Adrian employed were frequently African-American. Freddie Jenkins and Albert Nicholas led quartets there, as did the guitarist Bernard Addison. Occasionally there were white groups, including Wingy Manone's.)

Arthur Rollini (Adrian's brother and tenor saxophonist with Benny Goodman's band through the 1930s) told the author,

> I had the opportunity to hear Fats while he was working for Adrian at the Tap Room. I was with Goodman at the time, and we stayed upstairs in the President Hotel. Fats was a crowd-pleaser who played a heavy stride style on the upright piano,

and his voice was *à-propos* his style of playing. Customers constantly bought him shot glasses of whisky, which were lined up above the keyboard. Fats would consume these in great quantity, but with his great body frame, hardly showed any effect. [5]

After work at the Tap Room, Fats would still tour other nightspots, and in this way he came to recruit some of the sidemen for the Rhythm, the band with which he was to fulfill the Victor recording contract. Fats had no telephone at home, so (according to Harry Dial) he would call somebody else and ask them to do his telephoning for him. At the start, it is likely that Fats trusted much of the selection of sidemen to his bassist Billy Taylor (who had recorded with Fats before, as a member of McKinney's Cotton Pickers). He also asked his friend Bud Allen to get the men together for a one-off rehearsal at Fats's house before the first date.

Harry Dial, who played drums in the first session, has recounted his year with Fats in his autobiography, *All This Jazz About Jazz*, and recalls that Fats used to come regularly to Smalls' Paradise in Harlem, where he heard Harry playing in the house band. Although Harry was teetotal, Fats took a liking to him, and used to ask Mr. Smalls to let him off early so that he could join Fats and other musicians at the bar. Harry's musical abilities were not in doubt. Smalls' Paradise, like other Harlem nightclubs, used to put on a full show, and Harry (who was a trained musician and later worked as a copyist for the arranger Edgar Sampson) was one of the few drummers who could sight-read complicated show parts. He told the author in October 1986:

Drummers coming in with new bands, they couldn't play the show. Couldn't play the music. All because they couldn't read music, as the show wasn't that hard. So I came in, and at one rehearsal I'd play all that music, just like that. Now at that time, the union law was you had to be in a place six months before you could take a regular job. I hadn't been there six months, when I started. But Mr. Smalls got me in the union. Now a couple of the guys in the band didn't like me, because I kept telling them how rotten the band was, and they wanted to get me out. And finally, they succeeded. I had put my notice in a week before Mr. Smalls heard. Mr. Smalls called the bandleader: "All the trouble we had getting a drummer, and you want to let this man go?" He said to me, "You want to work here?"

I said, "Where else am I goin' to work?" Because I didn't see I'd get a job any place else. So Mr. Smalls issued an ultimatum: "Either you keep this man on the job, or you can take all of them out of here." So I stayed.[6]

And so during most of the time he was with the Rhythm, Harry was working at Smalls', or in the relief band at the Cotton Club, or with Dicky Wells at the Log Cabin on 133rd Street.

Another member of the Rhythm was also recruited from Smalls'. The trumpeter Herman Autrey had only recently moved from Philadelphia, where he had worked in the pit orchestra at the Standard Theater and later with Doc Hyder's band. (Once more this demonstrates the strong theatrical and show tradition that ran through the mid-1930s Harlem jazz scene.) In New York he joined Charlie Johnson's orchestra – a band that had a reputation for talent spotting – and he went with Johnson to Smalls' Paradise. "One night Fats Waller came in and listened to me for quite a while. Then a guy came up to me and said, 'Hey, Herman, you're in luck! Fats wants to know if you would like to make a record with him.' I hadn't made any records before, but I agreed to try it."

In an interview with Hugues Panassié in 1955, Autrey confirms that it was Billy Taylor who approached him to join the recording group. But Autrey (in George W. Kay's 1969 interview with him) didn't recall the rehearsal that Dial is sure took place at Fats's house. He says he was asked to report "the next morning" at 8 am.[7] This seems to me like artistic license on Autrey's part, since we know from the Victor time sheets that the first recording session of Fats and his Rhythm took place at 1.30 pm on Wednesday May 16, 1934. But it is a tribute to Autrey's talents that Fats picked him out, since the other two trumpeters in Johnson's band were Frankie Newton and Kenneth Roane, both very gifted players.

The fourth sideman in the Rhythm was still in school at the time of the first recordings by the band. Eighteen-year-old Al Casey was attending DeWitt Clinton High School. He had grown up in Kentucky, and then moved north with his family. When I talked to him in his Manhattan apartment, he told me:

> I had three uncles and an aunt who were in the singing group called the Southern Suns. They did pretty well and they even came to perform in New York. They knew Fats, because they'd worked with him in Cincinnati on his radio program. That show could be heard here in New York, because it had a very powerful transmitter. So when he left Cincinnati and came back to New York, they came and worked with him on the radio here too, on one of the AM stations. Then they decided to bring me to New York.
>
> Well, when I got here, he remembered me from Cincinnati. So the group took me to Fats's house, up on Edgecombe Avenue, I believe it was. They said, "He plays a little guitar."
>
> So Fats said, "Well, come again and bring your guitar and play a little bit."
>
> This would have been around 1933. It was like an audition, and I didn't really know what I was doing. But he said, "Okay! You're on my next date."
>
> And I did that record date for Victor, and thank God it caught on. Although I was still in school, I recorded with him after that on all the record dates with the new band. And then I got that feeling about wanting to go on the road, which you always get in music. And he said, "No! You show me a diploma, and then you can join me on the road." So although I did all the record dates, once the band became a regular thing, he took John Smith out on the road. One summer vacation, he did take me along, but just as a band boy, to get experience of being out with a group. But that wasn't until I'd graduated from High School.[8]

Al Casey: guitarist on many of Fats's best recordings.

Al (who at one time harbored ambitions to become an architect) became a full-time musician as soon as his studies were over.

The final member of the first recording group was the clarinet and saxophone player Ben Whittet, but the recording director of Victor, Eli Oberstein, didn't take to his rather stiff playing, and he was quickly replaced by Gene Sedric. Nevertheless, on May 16, 1934 the band took to the studios. Rehearsal or not, it appears that they didn't know which tunes were to be recorded until they got there. Harry Dial recalled:

> When we went in the studio, we had no idea what we were going to make. We made them four tunes and all we had seen first was piano parts. We knew them piano parts, everyone had piano parts. A lot of people don't believe we didn't have full arrangements, especially when you consider a number like *Serenade for a Wealthy Widow* [recorded at the third session in

September 1934]. We didn't have no arrangement, and the horns didn't even have a lead sheet. The other guys used the piano part and Fats, Al, and the bass player had to transpose. Fats would run through everything first. He ran through 'cos he vocalized on everything. He was phenomenal. He'd sit down, never having heard a composition, and play it. He'd play it and then sing it like he'd been doing it for six months.[9]

Other Waller sidemen interviewed at various times have confirmed this apparent spontaneity with which Fats approached the material he was to record. Bill Coleman, the trumpeter who took Autrey's place for a couple of sessions, said "it wasn't until he arrived in the studio that he was shown the themes chosen by the company." Waller would run over them "several times on the piano, making a mental plan for the piece and deciding when solos by Sedric or me would appear."[10]

If one listens carefully to the output of the band, it is possible to see that Fats had devised a number of cunning strategies to make the studio performances sound more polished and organized than they actually were. We know from Leonard Feather that he once found Fats in a rehearsal studio before a recording session furiously practicing his own solo for one of the pieces that was to be recorded. Part of the art of stride piano is to dazzle listeners with familiar patterns (or more frequently clichés) executed with stunning precision in unlikely places. As in many kinds of jazz, wittily placed quotations from other tunes are introduced to delight those listeners in the know. Many of Fats's best solos are likely to have been carefully constructed set pieces, or passages from such set pieces integrated with the unfamiliar structures of the tunes that Victor asked him to record.

Often Fats grafted a set introduction onto a tune. So, for instance, the two quite different tunes *Believe It Beloved* and *What's the Reason*, recorded five months apart, have an identical introduction, with a single string guitar motif repeated over a piano accompaniment.

Another technique Fats used was to bring a really unusual tone color into his introductions, or into the first instrumental run through the tune. Sometimes this would be an adaptation of a stage gimmick in which Fats played the tune on the bell-like celesta with his right hand, and accompanied himself at the piano with his left. On other occasions, he would state the melody on the piano over chords played on the vibraphone by another member of the band (such as the drummers Harry Dial or, later, Slick Jones). The March 1935 *Rosetta* is a perfect example of the first of these. The vocal version of this familiar tune by Earl Hines and Henri Woode is taken unusually slowly, and features a very carefully worked out introduction and ending. To disguise the fact that there isn't much of an arrangement to speak of, Fats introduces the celesta, which, coupled with the slow tempo (allowing the tune to be played through only a few times within the confines of a three-and-a-half-minute 78 rpm record), makes the recording sound like a well-thought-out routine. In *I Ain't Got Nobody*, from the same session, Fats plays a phenomenally difficult series of cascading runs over a guitar accompaniment. This is a classic example of set-piece piano playing being introduced to enliven what becomes more or less a "jam-session" version of the tune.

Such devices were the stock in trade of a musician used to presenting a variety of unfamiliar music to a live radio audience several nights a week. To his sidemen, more familiar (at least in the early days of the Rhythm) with work on the club circuit, Fats's abilities in the studio must have seemed remarkable. Nevertheless, with the benefit of hindsight, some of them were able to be critical of what went on. Gene Sedric, in an interview with Madeleine Gautier for the *Bulletin du Hot Club de France* in 1953, said, "Not one disc among all those that he made truly does him justice." He went on to say that Fats's recorded legacy doesn't give a real idea of his capabilities as a pianist. He also suggests that it was the fact that audiences seemed oblivious to Fats's remarkable piano playing that drove him to drink.

Fats didn't think of himself as a singer ... but with a bottle on the floor next to him, he'd sing and accompany himself at the piano. The people preferred this – and so did the managers. So, when they made him record all those discs with singing, which brought in plenty of money for everyone (and by no means a negligible amount), I'm sure that Fats didn't do all that he could have done.[11]

Nevertheless, the other view is equally valid. It is quite remarkable how many gems there are, even in the most Tin Pan Alley-like of Fats's recordings, and his skill on radio and in the recording studio is immediately apparent in the effective way that he used head arrangements and the tricks of his trade to make the most mundane material sound fully worked out. There may not be too many choruses of the glorious stride piano of which he was capable on the majority of his band sides (although there are some very fine ones indeed) but there are countless examples of skilled musicianship underlying the funny vocals and the lampooning.

Before looking at the development of the Rhythm into a road band and a part-time big band, it is worth examining what we know of its career in the studios, since it is possible to discover a lot about the recording industry in the mid-1930s by exploring what went on. The first recordings by the band were made in the 23rd Street studio of Victor in Manhattan. The other regular studio in the early years was the former Trinity Church at 114 North 5th Street, Camden, New Jersey. The Camden site was a favorite for Fats because it contained the old church organ. This allowed him to use the organ with the band (as he had in the late 1920s with Fletcher Henderson and with the Louisiana Sugar Babes). The instrument was a modified Estey church organ, which had been rebuilt in 1925–6 to incorporate many theater organ features. (Full details of this are given in Paul Machlin's *Stride*.)

Camden was a favorite with the sidemen for a different reason, despite the fact that they had to undertake a long train journey from

Gene Sedric.

Penn Station to Philadelphia and on to Camden. "I always liked to go," said Harry Dial, "because that was a $100 deal, whereas those other sessions on 23rd Street were just $20." In fact, the band started its career on even less. "We made our first date (or should I call it audition) for $13.50," Herman Autrey recalled. "But we got a $3 raise on our next date – then things began to happen."[12]

The biggest potential problem with Camden was that of time lag. When Garvin Bushell recorded there with the Louisiana Sugar Babes, he recollected that he and Jabbo Smith had stood at one end with James P. Johnson at the piano, while Fats had been perched "about a city block" away at the organ console. In that session, the rhythmic impetus was never carried by the organ – or at least never for very long. Instead the session developed into a series of duets, with Bushell's exciting clarinet or Jabbo's cornet carrying the rhythmic thrust of each piece over Fats's soft organ chords, and when the soloists laid back, James P. picked up the momentum at the more percussive piano.

We can't be quite sure how far the Rhythm were set up from the console when they recorded there in January 1935, but the balance on those numbers where the organ was used distinctly favors the bass, drums, and guitar. In this way, even though the sheer size of the organ and the placement of its pipes over a large area led to a time delay, the movement of the band is not dependent on Fats.

As well as musical difficulties, Camden recording dates did lead to one or two other problems for Fats's sidemen. Bill Coleman recalled that for the long train journey Fats had equipped himself with a couple of bottles of whisky. Waller was most generous with the supplies, and "wouldn't take a cent from any of us for all the refreshment. When he had taken a nip, he passed us the bottle, and the journey passed very agreeably." Once they got there, drinks were served between each recording. When the organ broke down during the recording of *Night Wind*, a full meal was served on the house. The train journey home was also an opportunity to polish off a couple of bottles of whisky. Bill didn't feel particularly intoxicated, but on the bandstand that night at the Ubangi Club, with Teddy Hill's band, "I couldn't even play eight measures . . . my brain wasn't working, my fingers wouldn't budge, and my eyesight was hazy."[13] The lesson to be learnt was not to try to drink as much as Fats. For all that, the session of January 5, 1935 was remarkably productive. It took place from 10.15 am until 4.45 pm, with an interval (presumably when the organ broke down, and the band had lunch) between 12.15 and 1.15. In that time fourteen sides were recorded, and all but six were issued. Of the eight which were released, *Baby Brown* and *I'm a Hundred Percent for You* were made in both instrumental and vocal versions.

Instrumental recordings were something the band was required to make from time to time. Sometimes the vocal and instrumental versions were virtually identical arrangements, but on other occasions the two could be radically different. When this happened, for instance in the two versions of *What's the Reason* from March 6, 1935, Fats's radio skills came to the fore again. In the instrumental version, what is virtually a jam session on the tune with bass and guitar solos is made by

Bill Coleman at the time of his recordings for Fats Waller.

changes of color to sound like an entirely different arrangement; Fats himself introduces the tune on celesta, while Herman Autrey takes a plunger mute solo, in direct contrast to his "open" solo on the vocal version. "Eli Oberstein (the recording director) wanted the instrumentals," said Harry Dial, "with one instrumental, one vocal version of the same thing, because he figured the band was good enough for him to issue some instrumental recordings."[14]

The majority of the sessions recorded by the Rhythm were not made at Camden, but at the Victor Studios in New York City. During the band's nine-year recording life, a number of technical changes occurred. While in terms of major new innovations 1934 to 1943 was essentially a static period in the history of sound recording, the time was one of increasing development and sophistication. The first electric recordings had been made in 1925, but while electric microphones and amplifiers contributed to the fidelity of the sound, the recording medium was still the "direct cut" disc. The standard was the 78 rpm record, and it was not until 1948 that Columbia introduced the long-playing $33\frac{1}{3}$ record. In 1949 the 45 rpm single was pioneered by RCA.

The survival of items filling more than the three-and-a-half-minute 78 rpm disc is largely a consequence of Fats's prodigious recording activity and popularity. There is a small body of material recorded for the Muzak Corporation on slower speed long-playing "transcription discs." On these, recorded with the intention of providing background or "dial-a-disc" entertainment, Hugues Panassié (who heard Fats in person many times) wrote: "These discs were the only ones in which I can clearly hear his true vocal timbre, with both the warmth and tenderness which are so frequently missing from his recordings."[15] Another body of extant recorded material consists of the surprisingly large number of Fats's broadcasts that have survived. Particularly as these broadcasts offer the opportunity to compare the band "live" with commercial recordings of the same material, they show just how

The line-up from Waller's March 11, 1938 session photographed in an informal setting.

professional an outfit Fats's band was in the recording studio and its ability to compress the songs into tightly wrought versions, perfect for the form of the 78 rpm disc. (The broadcasts were generally recorded either on glass acetate discs, or on the magnetic wire recorder, a precursor of the tape recorder, which was developed in the USA during the 1930s by Bell Laboratories and Brush Soundmirror.)

In the years from the first sessions by the Rhythm until its final Victor dates at the start of the 1940s, there were various subtle improvements in the recording technology that was used. Accounts from the band members suggest that on the earliest sessions they were grouped around a single microphone, with a second one for Waller alone. And, as we shall discover shortly from drummer Harry Dial, some of the engineers' anxieties of the 1920s about recording full sets of drums meant that even as late as 1934 some bands were still being recorded with scaled-down kits.

By the 1940s, multiple microphones were in use. In a 1941 photograph, Fats is separately miked from the rest of the band. The microphones, hung on giant retort stands, are adjustable for height, and capable of being hung away from the stand by rather cumbersome counterweighted booms. Fats, who is pictured playing both Hammond organ (or celesta) and piano, has a mike hung above the junction of the two keyboards, and positioned to catch his vocals. The piano lid remains open (in the direction away from the mike), not having to be shut to avoid drowning the other bandsmen, who are grouped around a second microphone stand. Al Casey is nearest to it and bass player Cedric Wallace is between him and Slick Jones, who is using the full kit of drums.

The following year, the widely photographed session with the Deep River Boys vocal group shows that still further developments have taken place, and separate ribbon mikes are suspended from the ceiling for singers, piano, Fats's vocals, and the rest of the band. Drummer Arthur Trappier has his whole kit placed centrally on a platform in the area between the various microphones.

Remarkably enough, Fats's earliest sessions with the Rhythm were

The 1942 session with the Deep River Boys.

recorded with Harry Dial and his kit of drums similarly placed. Harry's control was such that he could use all his drums without likelihood of destroying the balance of the band. His bass drum can be heard clearly on the March and May 1935 sessions on such tracks as *Oh Susannah*, *Hate to Talk about Myself*, and *You're the Cutest One*.

All these sides, of course, would most probably have been recorded with band musicians grouped around the single microphone I have described. So Harry's technique is the more remarkable. He told me:

> I was using brushes most of the time, although I had the cymbals in the studio. They were there. I put 'em up, but most of the time I didn't play on them. I didn't need to. I used a bass drum on the recordings, too. Not only was I using the bass drum – I had the whole kit. Oberstein set me on a platform. I did it without padding or anything, and so that I could be picked up sufficiently, Oberstein set me on a platform right in the center of the band. That's the way we recorded. Usually they put the drummer away in the corner. Away in another city, I used to call it.[16]

Much of this chapter has concentrated on the cross-fertilization between Fats's radio and recording work. In a more general way, there was an organizational tie-up between the two. In 1929, Victor and RCA had merged. The year before, RCA had acquired the two big theater chains Keith and Orpheum. It became possible for one promotional management to control an artist's radio, recording, and stage careers. And so it was with Fats. Indeed, CBS radio had caused him to terminate the Tap Room engagement, which they felt was a conflict of interest with his twice-weekly radio show.

In late 1934, however, as the recording career of the Rhythm got under way, executives of CBS and Victor came together to promote Fats's band as a touring outfit. The first tour in early 1935 featured a band based on the six-piece recording group. It is quite difficult to define the "recording group," since for the whole of the first year of its life there was at least one change in the personnel for each session. However, practically speaking, it was generally understood to be Herman Autrey (trumpet, replaced by Bill Coleman only because of an engagement at the Apollo Theater which Autrey couldn't break), Gene Sedric (clarinet and tenor sax), Al Casey (guitar), Charlie Turner (bass, replacing Billy Taylor who joined Duke Ellington in early 1935), Harry Dial (drums), and Fats himself.

For the first tour, the line-up of the six-piece "core" of the band was Autrey, Turner, Casey (who would have been replaced as it was term-time by James Smith), Dial, and Waller, with Emmett Mathews on clarinet and saxophones. Sedric had a good job at a club on Long Island with Broadway Jones, and couldn't afford to give it up. The band started at Frank Daley's Meadow Brook Theater at Pompton Lakes, New Jersey, and went on up through New England to venues in Boston and Providence. After playing Philadelphia, the band ended up at the Apollo in Harlem for the week of February 22, 1935.

Although Harry Dial insisted both in his autobiography and in interviews with the author that this first tour was undertaken by the Victor recording band alone, other accounts (principally Maurice Waller's memoir of his father) suggest that from the outset the group

Fats with Al Casey (guitar) and Cedric Wallace (bass).

was expanded to a big band. Dial was adamant that the big band was a slightly later development. This confusion arises from the fact that the group was expanded to fourteen pieces for its week at the Apollo. The extra musicians were largely drawn from the band led by the bass player Charlie Turner. Once it had been formed, for this event, the big band toured frequently. The personnel given in Maurice Waller's book is based on published listings for the recording session of December 1935 – the first visit to the studio by the bigger group.

The band was slightly different when first enlarged. The trumpets are likely to have been Autrey, Joe Thomas, and Clarence Smith; the reeds were Sedric, Allen Jackson, and Rudy Powell; trombone was George Wilson; guitar, James Smith; Turner was on bass, Fats on piano, and Hank Duncan (from Turner's band) played second piano. Arrangements were by Alex Hill and Rudy Powell.

By the time the big band came to record, it had Sidney De Paris among the trumpets, Benny Morton on trombone, and the reed players Powell, Don Redman, Bob Carroll, and Edward Inge. At least that was conventionally accepted to be the personnel. But we know from Harry Dial (whose chair had been taken by the end of 1935 by Yank Porter) that Emmett Mathews often replaced Sedric in the band. Whilst Sedric is undeniably present on the records, the Swiss researcher Johnny Simmen has put forward the view that the searing soprano saxophone work which is such an exciting feature of the big band's first records is that of Emmett Mathews, and that he, rather than Inge, is present. This view is now endorsed by most discographers, including Brian Rust.

Mention of Johnny Simmen is important here, in that he reminds us in his feature on Hank Duncan (published in *Jazz Journal* in 1969) about the "cutting contests" that would form a nightly feature of the band's show in which Waller and Duncan would try to outplay one another. The band's recording of *I Got Rhythm* is an attempt to capture this part of the act on disc. Not many pianists would be up to the challenge, but Hank Duncan was, and although the recording balance favors Waller it is still possible to hear what worthy opponents the two men were for one another.

Harry Dial remembers that Hank would play throughout each gig. If they were at a theater, then he would play "the show," leaving Fats to come on for the "band specialties," during which they would both be heard. On ordinary club or dance dates, there were two pianos all evening. When it came to the cutting contest, Harry recalled, Fats would suddenly shout, "I've got to get him! I've got to get him!" and they would launch into the full routine. The recording band had the advantage of an outstanding rhythm section. Not only was there "Brother Duncan" at the second piano, but Yank Porter had a legendary reputation in Harlem as the drummer who was brought in to "save the show." Danny and Blue Lu Barker told the author how Harlem producers would be worried about the sound of a house or show band for a revue. "Send for Yank Porter," they'd say, and his legendary ability to hold a pit orchestra together and to read a difficult score (a skill he shared with Harry Dial) would pull the show round from mediocrity to success.

When some big bands of the period went on the road, they took with them an elaborate show. Danny Barker talks of his band travels

Fats Waller and his Rhythm, 1941. Slick Jones (drums), Cedric Wallace (bass), Gene Sedric (reeds), and John Hamilton (trumpet).

with Cab Calloway's orchestra and the Cotton Club Revue; Calloway's band traveled by train, or in buses which were relatively luxurious for the period. Ellington's band traveled in private Pullmans. To start with, Fats's band did not aspire to such dizzy heights: they traveled by band bus (known as "Old Methuselah") to a string of one-nighters. There were no added singers or dancers. "We were the show," said Harry Dial. "But then Fats was a show all by himself."[17]

In a year, therefore, from 1934 to 1935, Fats had come back from appearing as a soloist on a Midwest radio show to lead a band whose record sales were doing well, and which was able to undertake extended tours. Although there were difficulties (from Fats's alimony payments running into arrears to skipped bookings leading to lawsuits), although he was occasionally absent on the West Coast or in Europe, and although Fats changed manager (from Phil Ponce to Ed Kirkeby), the fundamental pattern of the last nine years of Waller's life was bound up with the Rhythm and the big band. While the big band made only four sets of recordings in the commercial studios – in December 1935, April 1938, July 1941, and March 1942

— it was formed for several months of most years. Sidemen came and went, but the core of the band, the six-piece recording group, stayed remarkably consistent.

To hear what it was like being part of the touring group gives a valuable insight into the life on the road of a "name" band in the 1930s. "I don't think we was ever gone more than four or five weeks," recalled Harry Dial, "but on those strings of one-nighters you got to sleep on the bus, and it was terrible, awful."[18]

Joe Thomas, the trumpeter, remembered that, to make the long bus journeys bearable, Fats resorted to the same brand of liquid anesthetic that Bill Coleman experienced on the train to Camden. Shortly after leaving Fats's 118th Street house, there was a thirty-minute wait for a van bringing a case of whisky. "Each guy receives a quart. 'Everybody straight?' Fats calls out. Everybody is. 'Well,' he announces, 'Don't bother me for the rest of the trip.'" Joe Thomas is also the source of one of many stories about Fats entering a restaurant and ordering steak for two and chicken for two. When asked where the other members of his party were, Fats's standard reply came straight back: "Ain't nobody here but me, honey!"

Stories of Fats's generosity to his sidemen and others were legion. Autrey recalls being bought an expensive new trumpet. Herb Flemming, trombonist with the later big bands, was told by Fats to go and replace his old trombone. Herb and the salesman turned up at the theater with a new instrument, to find Fats winning at cards. The winnings were presented to Flemming, and Fats instructed him to try the horn "and let me hear what $325 sounds like."

On the other hand Flemming recalls Fats turning up for a band "meet" at Grand Central Station with ankles so swollen he could barely lace his shoes. The band tried to get him to put off the date, but his reaction was characteristic: "Get on the train, fellows. I've got to eat, and so have you and your families ... let's get on with it."[19]

In later years, the band did aspire to its own private rail coach, and as Fats grew in popularity, he assembled a show around himself and the band with a troupe of about sixteen girls. He was famed for his capacities as an eater, drinker, and womanizer. None of Fats's sidemen to whom the author has talked has ever been critical of him, however. All of them remember his magnanimity, his good humor, and his open-heartedness.

There is, however, one recurrent type of story that suggests Fats could take things too far. Typical of this is the recollection of one of his sidemen concerning a tour during which a riotous party was in progress one evening after the show. Someone noticed that John "Bugs" Hamilton, the trumpeter, was missing. He was found sitting on the step of the locked band bus, weeping with fatigue, asking to be let on the bus to sleep. Fats's reaction was typical. Pointing at the party, he announced, "Get back in there and enjoy yourself!"

There are several similar stories concerning Fats's tastes for involving all and sundry in excessive partying. He is said (while in England) to have telephoned Nat Gonella at three in the morning to inquire why he was not at the party that was going on in Waller's hotel room. His own trumpeter, Herman Autrey, told a Canadian interviewer: "[Fats] told me I ate and slept too much, but I said 'Fats, I'm just human, I have to eat and sleep.' It was too much for me to keep up."[20]

John "Bugs" Hamilton.

In addition to developing his tastes for staying up all night at parties, excessive road touring had another effect on Fats: he would suddenly (despite all professional instincts) harbor an irrational desire to return home to New York. While this happened most often during the 1937–8 season (following which Ed Kirkeby booked Waller's first European tour to find new management not yet prejudiced against Fats on account of his reputation for skipping gigs), it had its origins in the very first band tour of the Rhythm. Harry Dial told the author:

> We were on our way someplace, a one-nighter, guess we were halfway there. So Fats told the driver: "Turn this jalopy around! Let's head back to New York." Well, we all started looking at one another. All we were thinking about was the money. Fats looked round and saw all these long faces, so he got up and paid everybody off, and the smiles came back. Somebody asked him what the matter was – he said "Huh! That guy said something I didn't like last time I was up here."[21]

Musically, despite the stories of missed gigs, rows over poor pianos, and (at least to start with) poor traveling conditions, when it actually played the band was run on stage with Fats's by now well-developed professionalism. A member of the big band wrote in to John McLellan's jazz column in the *Boston Traveler* in December 1957 to recall how the stage appearances were run.

> Since the small group was the nucleus of the larger, he'd often start with one of his recordings made with the small group, without telling us what he was doing. We knew instinctively under such circumstances that everyone but the small group was to lay out and let them carry the ball.
> When playing some of the current favorites, he might, when he came to the end of an arrangement, insist on some extra choruses ... and he often called for the blues in a certain key, especially B-flat. He often sang in that key. He had an extensive

musical library, and always ... with the big band, took heavily from it for music for the band. There were certain head arrangements (compiled by the band and never written down) which were better than the written ones, but they went exactly according to formula.[22]

All this gives us a good picture of Fats as a bandleader during the period of his greatest popularity. The vast corpus of his recordings is a testimony to his development in nine years. This, plus the issue of so much of his broadcast material from his residencies at the New York Yacht Club and the Panther Room at Chicago's Sherman Hotel, coupled with the extended Muzak recordings, makes it possible to build up a detailed sound portrait of his work with the Rhythm and big band, both in three-and-a-half-minute cameos on 78 rpm disc, and in a more relaxed and extended vein.

Hamilton, Wallace, and Sedric (back to camera) with a dancer in one of Fats's films.

FILMS

Shortly after the first tour by Fats Waller and his Rhythm in early 1935, the combination of growing record sales and the reputation of his band led to Waller's being invited to go to Hollywood to make a picture for RKO entitled *Hooray for Love!* Fats journeyed all the way there for one day's work on the film, in which he appeared with the dancer Bill "Bojangles" Robinson. Ironically, the same pairing of Waller and Robinson was to be a feature of Fats's final film made in 1943 – *Stormy Weather*.

Bojangles had made his reputation as a dancer and cabaret entertainer, and had a particular connection with clubs in Harlem. Born in 1878, he had appeared as a child dancer in restaurants and in vaudeville as what was known as a "pickaninny" (the term was widely applied to African-American child entertainers with the troupes traveling on the TOBA circuit), and he later became something of a star attraction on the major touring circuits of Keith and Orpheum. Robinson was a particularly skilled tap dancer, and while dancing on his toes (a particular innovation of his) and performing his specialties such as dancing up and down staircases, he was apt to tell anecdotes and comment humorously on his feet and events going on around him. According to Danny Barker, Robinson was very active in Harlem politics, and arranged political rallies with other notables such as Walter White and Miss Mary McLeod Bethune. Danny recalls Robinson, like Jelly Roll Morton, as a man who salivated while he talked, spurts of "mouth juice" showering the people with whom he was engaged in conversation. Danny experienced Bill auditioning acts for the Cotton Club, in partnership with Cab Calloway, whose band enjoyed a residency there in the mid-1930s after Duke Ellington left the club.

Perhaps because of his connection with Harlem clubland alone, Robinson was a particularly suitable character to feature in Walter Lang's film. It was an adaptation of a stage musical comedy, presented as the story of the rehearsals and performances of the show. Who better to team up with Robinson and to appear in a couple of feature numbers than the other man of the Harlem club scene and the musical theater, Fats Waller?

In the film Fats sang *I'm Livin' in a Great Big Way*. For many years this was available only on the soundtrack, but it was eventually issued on LP in the 1980s. There is some controversy about the actual recording date of this track, but it took place sometime between the beginning of March and early May, when Waller was back in New York. What is certain, however, is that Fats made two visits to Hollywood in 1935, the second to make a picture for 20th Century Fox called *King of Burlesque*.

In the earlier film, *Hooray for Love!*, other musicians who appeared included a contingent from Les Hite's orchestra. Fats played a short engagement with them from March 26 at the New Cotton Club in Culver City, run by Frank Sebastian. This cabaret was situated across the street from the MGM film lot, and had a house band which since 1930 had been run by Hite, a saxophonist whom the management had brought in to back Louis Armstrong. Armstrong's stay had not been without drama, as he was arrested on a drugs charge while playing there. Nevertheless, Armstrong had molded the Hite group into a first-rate band, and they had made a number of excellent recordings between October 1930 and March 1931. After Louis's departure,

Fats in *King of Burlesque.*

Hite's band continued to work regularly, and many of the sidemen also doubled as studio musicians in the growing industry of supplying music for sound pictures.

Buck Clayton, who worked on the West Coast with Charlie Echols's orchestra, as well as with his own band, heard Louis with the Hite orchestra, and remembers later hearing Fats Waller with the same band. He recalled, "Fats Waller came to the Cotton Club after Louis and was a success also, but I don't think anyone in the world could have had the success that Pops had. Fats was funny, jolly, and one hell of a pianist and did very well in Los Angeles.[1]

There is no doubt that Fats enjoyed life in Los Angeles and Hollywood with his usual great capacity for high living. The actor-

.comedian Slim Thompson, who made many films in Hollywood, recollected Fats having the adjoining suite at the Dunbar Hotel, the main African-American show business hotel on Central Avenue, the center of the entertainment district.

> I recall there was a party in Fats's suite. The Three Rockets who were appearing at the Club Alabam, which was next door to the hotel, were at the party. They were Baby Face, Johnny Thomas and Andy. Buck Clayton was there and Art Tatum. There were chorus girls from the Club Alabam too. We were all drinking and having fun. Louis Armstrong was in Hollywood that year too, working on the film *Pennies from Heaven*. He and I would get together and work on his parts ... of course Pops was invited to the party, he loved Fats – and he wanted to be there – I could tell. But he sadly explained, "I'd love to make it but I have to get up at 6.00 am – to make some takes." ... What a party. We exchanged garments. The men put on the girls' clothes and the girls wore the men's clothes. Art Tatum put on a dress and broke it up, doing an imitation of Mary Lou Williams. Not to be outdone, Fats was dressed as Bessie Smith and really killed us, singing *See See Rider*. In the midst of the song, Fats stopped and said "Boy, I'm really riding, and Mary Lou you're not doin' so bad with the keys!"[2]

One of the best-known musicians on the West Coast musical scene was the trumpeter Teddy Buckner, and he appeared together with Fats in Waller's second film of 1935, *King of Burlesque*. In this picture Fats was cast as an elevator operator in the office building where Warner Baxter, who portrayed a theatrical producer down on his luck, needed help from Fats and other entertainers to rebuild his business as an agent and producer. In this film Fats sang *I've Got My Fingers Crossed*, as well as the songs *Too Good to Be True* and *Spreading Rhythm Around*.[3]

According to Ed Kirkeby, once *Hooray for Love!* was given its première in Philadelphia, Fats's band was booked to promote the film, enabling him to perform his well-known version of *I've Got My Fingers Crossed* from the stage in between his performances on the screen.[4] The Victor company cashed in on the popularity of *I've Got My Fingers Crossed*, and of *Spreading Rhythm Around* from the second film and, from a recording session in November 1935, issued the two back-to-back (Victor 25211). A few days later, Fats's big band made its celebrated recording in New York, including the cutting contest between Fats and Hank Duncan mentioned in the previous chapter.

After the end of 1935, Fats did not return to the film studios again until 1941, but this is not to say that he stayed away from the West Coast in the meantime. In 1937 he was booked into the Hollywood Famous Door, where he fronted the small band led by the bassist Al Morgan.

Morgan was a member of that great New Orleans family of musicians which is perhaps best known through the recordings of the band led by his brother Sam Morgan, one of the better 1920s groups not to have abandoned New Orleans for the lure of Chicago. Al himself was almost a one-man history of jazz. In the mid-1920s he had joined Fate Marable's band, working the riverboats from New Orleans up to St Louis and beyond to St Paul and Minneapolis. In that band he frequently worked alongside the bassist Pops Foster, and nobody exemplifies better than these two the strong four-to-the-bar slapping bass style of the New Orleans players who revolutionized the jazz rhythm section with their influential shift away from the tuba to the string bass. In 1929, with Lee Collins, Al had made recordings which are some of the finest ever created in the New Orleans genre; the same year, in New York, he had made his first recordings with Fats Waller in a band including Jack Teagarden and Gene Krupa. He had been a member of the famous Billy Banks Rhythmakers (though in an earlier version of that 1932 recording band than the one in which Fats himself appeared). Morgan had then gone on the road with Cab Calloway's big band. It was a great reunion for Al to be working with Fats Waller again, and he recalled that he performed in California with Fats for some three and a half months in 1937. He found it a pleasurable experience, and could remember no-one who was easier to work for. "I don't think anyone could get mad at Fats; as soon as he walked in, he transferred to you some of his warmth and humor, and you enjoyed every minute of the set."[5]

Another member of the same little band was Lee Young, the drummer brother of the famous saxophonist Lester Young. He told Valerie Wilmer,

> getting back to 1937: Fats Waller came to work at the Famous Door and we used to have great sessions every Sunday. Al Morgan was on bass, Paul Campbell (who later went with Basie) played trumpet, and Jerry Colonna would sometimes come out and play trombone. You know he wasn't fooling, he could really play. I was kind of excited about everything all the time, but Fats really was the most jovial and the most

Fats and the Rhythm in one of his "soundies."

pleasant man I've ever known. Oscar Peterson reminds me so much of him, though he doesn't drink like Fats did.

I made six records with Fats, Paul, Al and Caughey Roberts (who had just left Basie) on alto, and Ceele Burke on guitar.[6]

These recordings are a delight, since, made with the same instrumentation as Fats's normal band, they give a chance for one to hear completely different players and consequently a subtly different sound.

Fats Waller's next film appearances are part of an early 1940s phenomenon known as the "soundies." In many respects these were the forerunners of today's rock or pop videos. But given the social ethos of the 1940s, they were designed to run on public jukeboxes, which, in addition to playing a three-and-a-half-minute soundtrack (comparable to the playing time of a 78 rpm disc), also projected a film of the musicians via a complicated system of mirrors.

This jukebox was known as the Mills Panorama and was manufactured by a company called the RCM Corporation, whose initials were made up from the names of the three principals: James Roosevelt (the son of President Franklin D. Roosevelt), Sam Coslow (a songwriter), and Ralph Mills (the owner of a plant that had previously manufactured conventional sound jukeboxes). The company's aim was simple: it expected to extend the function of the jukebox so that customers in bars could see as well as hear their favorite performers.

It is likely that more than 1000 soundies were made, and despite the fact that in most instances the musicians mimed to a pre-recorded soundtrack, they remain a unique visual document of performances by many of the greatest stars of popular music. It is particularly interesting that their main period of production (from 1941 to 1947) overlapped with the ban on commercial recordings by the American Federation of Musicians (from 1942 to 1945). Consequently, apart from the V-discs, which were produced for the armed forces, the soundies are virtually the only body of sound recordings made during the World War II period by many musicians.

Title sequences (this and facing page) from two of the "soundies."

In many ways it was the war itself that curtailed the production of soundies. The changing social patterns of entertainment after the war, together with the emergence of television in the United States, led to a cessation of production. One of the more extraordinary features of soundies was that to correspond properly with the mirror projection system, the films themselves were printed in reverse. Printed the right way round, many of them found their way into television libraries and the collections of film buffs.

When Fats Waller went into the studios to make his four low-budget soundies in 1941, the industry was still in its infancy, and production was at its height (according to the film historian David Meeker) of five or six films per week. Customers paid a dime to see each film on the machine.[7]

The films show characteristic performances by Fats and his Rhythm (a version of the band that featured John Hamilton, trumpet; Gene Sedric, reeds; Al Casey, guitar; Cedric Wallace, bass; and Slick Jones, drums). On *The Joint Is Jumpin'* it is possible to see the vocalist

Myra Johnson, who frequently worked with Fats and his band in the early 1940s. In fact, the Waller band had often had a female vocalist: radio airshots include performances by Kay Perry; there are commercial duets between Waller and the singer and pianist Una Mae Carlisle (who was something of a protégée of Fats); and another singer who was featured with the band was the entertainer Jeni le Gon. Interestingly, it is she who dances with Fats and Bill Robinson in the feature song *I'm Livin' in a Great Big Way*, from the 1935 picture *Hooray for Love!* For many years she appeared as vocalist and dancer with Fats's band during the stage shows that ran between the screened performances of films at such movie houses as the Regal or Vendome theaters in Chicago, the Apollo in New York, the Howard in Washington, and (the scene of her final appearance with Fats in 1943) the Paramount in Los Angeles. She recalled:

> The stage show would last about an hour and a half. After the opening acts had done their turns, Fats would come on with his

group and remain for the rest of the show. It was during this last portion that Fats would introduce me. While I was known primarily as a dancer, my first number would be a vocal. Fats gave me four of his numbers to sing on the theater tour. They were *Humptey Dumptey, Here It Is, I Had To Do It*, and one other I can't recall now. ... Fats suggested these particular songs as he thought they would best suit me because I didn't profess to be a great singer. He also recommended that I used my singing as an opening as well as a relief for my routine because I danced very hard. I danced like a boy – I did flips and knee drops and toe stands and all that sort of business so, when I had to sing after I'd danced, he gave me these cute little numbers so that I could talk-sing.[8]

Inevitably Fats would interrupt these sweet vocals with his usual line of vocal patter, but more remarkably Jeni le Gon is sure that Fats would finish off the act by sharing a dance with her. We know from her accounts and those of others that he used to wrap the curtain round his body and shake his massive backside at the audience in perfect rhythm, but it is something of a surprise to learn that he would do very energetic dances with her. "He moved. He handled dancing almost as he did his piano. Remarkable when you think of his size."

The film historian Dave Dixon has speculated that there may once have been a few seconds of Fats dancing with the chorus girls in an uncut print of his soundie *Honeysuckle Rose*. All known prints of this film are cut in such a way that in mid-film he returns to the piano, as the chorus line is seen in the distance. It is highly likely that one of the scenes shot but discarded from the film included Fats's energetic dancing.[9]

The performances on Fats's four soundies are of two distinctly different types. There are relatively straightforward versions of his own compositions *Honeysuckle Rose* and *Ain't Misbehavin'*, while his comic jive song *Your Feet's Too Big* receives a treatment very similar to that on the commercial Victor recording, with some rather absurd dance sequences built around a man in outsize shoes. The final film,

Myra Johnson sings in *The Joint Is Jumpin'*.

Fats returns to the band after the dance sequence in *Honeysuckle Rose*.

The Joint Is Jumpin', is a piece of real mayhem, and not only replicates the sound of the commercial Victor recording, but goes some way towards the jive recordings later issued on soundies. There had always been an element of rhythm and blues about Fats's playing, but it is clearly apparent here. (The soundies were moving very much in the direction of 1940s rhythm and blues, and one of the most popular subjects for these later films was Louis Jordan.)

The final film in which Fats Waller was involved was made during the last year of his life, 1943, on the first of two visits that year to Hollywood.

Stormy Weather was a remarkable movie, made by William le Baron and directed by Andrew Stone. On a somewhat slender plot by Jerry Horwin and Seymour B. Robinson, the script was put together by Frederic Jackson, lyricist Ted Koehler, and H. S. Kraft. It was built around Bojangles Robinson, and celebrates his career in show business from 1911 to 1936, using spurious clippings from a magazine called *Theater World*. Bill Robinson's memory is jolted by the sight of various ads and tributes to stages in his career, and he acts as the page-turning link between a number of small but relatively unrelated scenes, all of which are built on musical performances. Fats performed *Ain't Misbehavin'* with a group whose instrumentation resembled that of his regular Rhythm, but including such luminaries as Benny Carter, Slam Stewart, and the drummer Zutty Singleton. The same group recorded Fats's song *Moppin' and Boppin'*, but unfortunately this was dropped from the film, though a fine soundtrack recording remains. With Ada Brown, Fats performed *That Ain't Right*, and other notable participants in the film include Cab Calloway and Lena Horne. The associate producer, or talent scout, for the film (who had assembled the great cast of performers) was the agent, entrepreneur, and publisher Irving Mills.

According to Ed Kirkeby, it was Mills who signed up Benny Carter and Fats to work together on writing *Moppin' and Boppin'*, and even though it was dropped from the film, he snapped up the publishing rights. The recording of the tune is remarkable, with one of the very

Benny Carter (who doubled on
alto saxophone, as here, and
trumpet).

finest drum solos (in his own opinion) ever recorded by Zutty
Singleton. The drums start the number, after Fats yells out, "You
want some more of that mess? Well here 'tis, Zutty, take over! Pour it
on them." Zutty then gives a tremendous demonstration of New
Orleans drumming, showing his prowess at obtaining a variety of tones
from every part of the drum kit. As the full band comes in, it is evident
what Fats might have achieved had he surrounded himself with
musicians of this caliber all the time. This is not to disparage the work
of the better musicians in his band – Bill Coleman, Herman Autrey,
Gene Sedric, Rudy Powell, and Al Casey – but it is immediately obvious
how a cohesive rhythm section anchored by a good four-to-the-bar bass
player and a genuine swinging drummer adds depth and vigor to the
performance of the whole band.

In many ways, too, *Moppin' and Boppin'* shows us the direction
that his jazz might have taken had Fats lived on into 1944. It is a

transitional number, with the full gamut of musical styles from early jazz to bebop and beyond. If Zutty's New Orleans style drums look back to the early days, if Benny Carter, Fats himself, and the saxophonist Eugene Porter typify the swing era, then Slam Stewart's bowed bass solo looks forward to bebop, and the similar work that he contributed to the earliest Charlie Parker–Dizzy Gillespie collaborations. Fats shows that he can be a profound accompanist in all these styles, and the tune shows just what a crossroads jazz had reached in 1943.

According to Gene Porter, interviewed in 1972 by Karl Gurt zur Heide, the keynote of Hollywood in 1943 was versatility. Porter worked generally with Benny Carter: "Benny and I worked in the studio band together – 20th Century Fox ... I didn't want solo work. I never did look for the limelight, you know, like a lot of the guys did. I was happy to be a section man." Porter talks about how his versatility kept him in demand for all kinds of session, and in addition to those with Fats, he made recordings with Dinah Washington, Ivie Anderson, and Jessie Price.[10]

Musical crossroads or not, the band in the film was presented in a

Fats, the film star.

Stormy Weather: Fats leads the band through *Ain't Misbehavin'* (left to right) Alton Moore (trombone); Zutty Singleton (drums); Irving Ashby (guitar, hidden); Benny Carter (trumpet); Slam Stewart (bass); Gene Porter (clarinet); Fats.

pastiche of a Harlem club, with Fats playing a battered upright piano, the hats of the others stacked on top of it, and a large jug placed in front of the band where members of the audience could contribute tips for the musicians. The legend "FEED THE KITTY" painted on the jug in capital letters made the point obvious. Slam Stewart stands in a corner behind Fats on the slightly raised stage, and Gene Porter and Benny Carter make up part of the front line with the guitarist Irving Ashby behind them. But the most dominant, significant musician in the front line is the hunched figure of the drummer Zutty Singleton, his drum kit at the front of the band replete with painted bass drum and all his trick effects from cowbells to ratchets and woodblocks. The trombonist

Alton Moore sits on the far side of the stage from Fats. The same band is joined by Ada Brown for *That Ain't Right*.

Fats was widely praised for his small acting part in the film, and for the quality of the musical performances, which more than held their own with those of other seasoned performers such as Lena Horne, Bojangles Robinson, and Cab Calloway. *Stormy Weather* was, in some respects, a triumph for the African-American musicians and artists involved, not least because it celebrated a panoply of African-American entertainment. It was a far cry from the walk-on part that Fats had as a lift man in *The King of Burlesque*, where he felt constrained to make his dialog less Uncle Tom-ish. It is a tragedy that more of Fats Waller's work is not preserved on film, but in the cross-section that survives from the bit parts and musical performances from 1935, the four soundies, and the crowning glory of the appearances in *Stormy Weather*, we at least have a legacy of quality and good humor from Fats in his guise as film performer. It is particularly sad that shortly before his death he announced in a radio interview with Hugh Conover (in September 1943) that there were plans afoot for him to follow up his major success in *Stormy Weather* with another film.

FATS IN EUROPE

Many major American jazz musicians toured in Europe after the inaugural performance at the Hammersmith Palais in London by the Original Dixieland Jazz Band in 1919. Notable among them were Sidney Bechet (who came with Will Marion Cook and stayed with small groups which also included Henry Saparo and Benny Peyton), Cab Calloway, and Duke Ellington.

Both the Calloway and Ellington bands were lucky enough to have toured in England and elsewhere in Europe as complete orchestras. However, in 1934 the English Musicians' Union refused to allow American bands to perform in Britain but was more relaxed concerning the regulations for solo variety artists. After 1934, therefore, most visiting American jazz artists appeared on the variety circuits, usually as solo performers backed by local musicians.

Fats Waller had made his first visit to Europe some two years before the English Musicians' Union ban, although he spent virtually the entire time in the Paris region. At the time there were reports that he was to come to London, but he apparently did not do so — returning directly to New York from Paris (according to some accounts because of homesickness, and to others "because of a consular difficulty" with the British authorities). The latter view was that expressed by

Hugues Panassié.

John Hammond in the *Melody Maker*, but most accounts concentrate on the fact that Fats, having come to Paris with his friend Spencer Williams, abandoned the latter in a restaurant, and was next found in New York!

In many respects the 1932 visit to France was nothing more than an extended holiday, in that Fats allegedly sat up all night with Williams writing more than twenty songs to pay for the fare and to provide some traveling expenses, and was not formally booked in advance to play any engagements during his stay in France. He did, while there, meet a number of local jazz fans and enthusiasts, notably the prime mover behind the Hot Club of France, Hugues Panassié, who committed his memories of Fats's visit to paper. Panassié confirms that most of Fats's stay was spent playing in nightclubs. In particular, he appeared at a place called La Rumba. Panassié remembered, "He was there from half an hour after midnight. I had nothing to complain of: he played a great deal, for he was equally fond of taking his part in an orchestra, and giving solos."[1]

Most of Panassié's article then becomes a critical review of Fats's playing, taking notice of his formidable keyboard attack and talking about his ability to keep one ear on a conversation and another on the house band which was playing at the same time.

But the Paris visit was really an irrelevance. As a professional artist, Fats was not to come to Europe on a properly organized tour until 1938, when his manager Ed Kirkeby set up a trip in conjunction with the management company Moss Empires Limited.

The principal reasons that American managements looked to Europe for their artists were to command high fees, and to break new ground for musicians already widely known in Europe through the medium of gramophone records. Before the Musicians' Union ban it had been an extremely successful device for the orchestras of Calloway and Ellington, and after the ban some American soloists continued to tour on the same basis – principal among them Louis

Armstrong, who came to Europe as an international star to front locally organized bands.

The European music scene was well aware of the talents of American jazz musicians, and a number of important individuals spent periods of time in Britain and continental Europe during the 1930s. Perhaps the most famous of these was Benny Carter (the alto saxophonist and trumpeter), who was retained as a staff arranger by the BBC in London from 1936 onwards. The American clarinetist Danny Polo was also based in London and made a number of

Fats and Anita.

significant recordings, as did the visiting saxophonist Coleman Hawkins, who appeared with a number of bands in Britain and on the continent.

Fats, therefore, was to integrate himself into an already established scene for visiting Americans.

At the point of his departure, in July 1938, Fats had become a difficult proposition for his manager Ed Kirkeby to sell in America. He had had a particularly bad string of one-night engagements, and had exhausted the theater circuit.

Kirkeby contacted Tommy Rockwell (the man who had arranged Armstrong's European tour, and who had also booked the Mills Brothers into English theaters) and asked him to cable the Moss organization to find out if they would take Fats Waller for a ten-week tour as a single, at a salary of $2500 per week. To everybody's apparent surprise, the English management agreed.

In 1938, the English provincial theater circuit was run by a number of managements, some of whom survived into the late twentieth century. Most of these management companies administered a number of important theaters. The General Theatre Corporation administered the Birmingham Hippodrome, the Brighton Hippodrome, the Holborn Empire, the Palladium, the Penge Empire, the Portsmouth Hippodrome, and the Wolverhampton Hippodrome; Howard and Wyndhams looked after the Birmingham Prince of Wales Theatre, the Edinburgh King's and Lyceum theaters, the Manchester Opera House, and the Newcastle Theatre Royal. The Stoll Corporation ran the Chiswick Empire, the Hackney Empire, the Leicester Palladium, the Glasgow King's and Royal theaters, the Manchester Hippodrome, the Shepherd's Bush Empire, and the Wood Green Empire. By far the largest organization, however, was the Moss Empires group, which ran theaters from Scotland to the South Coast, notably the Birmingham Empire, the Bradford Alhambra, the Edinburgh Empire, the Finsbury Park Empire, the Glasgow Alhambra and Empire, and the Leeds Empire and Royal theaters – as well as many others. The Moss group took the head contract for Fats Waller, although he also appeared at a number of theaters operated by the other management corporations.

At the time he arrived (July 1938), Fats was by no means the only jazz or African-American act to be touring the English variety circuit. The singer Josephine Baker, who had been such a great hit in *La Revue nègre* in Paris and London in the mid-1920s, had been headlining at the Palladium during June 1938. Similarly, Django Reinhardt and Stephane Grappelli were touring the same circuit during July and August.

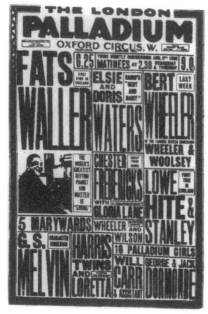

Poster for Fats at the Palladium during his first week there, August 1938.

Fats traveled with his wife Anita and Ed Kirkeby aboard the S.S. *Transylvania* of the Anchor Line and arrived at Greenock, near Glasgow, on July 29. He was greeted at the dockside by Billy Mason's Empirex Orchestra, a band which had been put together for the 1938 Empire Exhibition in Glasgow. Within two days of his arrival Fats opened at the Glasgow Empire Theatre. The other acts on the bill underline the fact that he was very much part of a variety group, finding himself alongside Jimmy James, Chester Fredericks and Gloria Lane,

Senatel Murphy, Ross and Bennett, Freddie Bamburger, the Mito Trio, Damsel and Lady, Power and Page, and Budd Cordell. This was the most out-and-out variety show playing in Glasgow at the time. Among other presentations in the city were *Tom Arnold's Revels* at the Alhambra, a season of serious plays at the Glasgow Royal, and the show *Half Past Eight* at the King's Theatre. While the last named was variety, strictly speaking, it was nevertheless organized around a loose plot, which was noticeably absent from Fats's variety show.

Fats's appearance at the Glasgow Empire was greeted with rapture by the local critics. Ed Kirkeby quotes the extremely encouraging review from the *Glasgow Evening News*, which referred to the "dynamic 285 lb King of Swing." Fats's act concentrated on a relatively straight performance of *Loch Lomond* as well as the more predictable Waller swing tunes *Honeysuckle Rose*, *Handful of Keys*, *Ain't Misbehavin'*, and *I'm Gonna Sit Right Down and Write Myself a Letter*. According to Kirkeby, Fats took ten curtain calls on his first night.

The London magazine *The Stage* was a little less enthusiastic in its report, but the Glasgow correspondent noted, "Fats Waller, a rhythm pianist, scores in his swing numbers, old and new."[2]

It was not until the next week, when Fats arrived at the London Palladium, that he really came to the notice of the public: the review in *The Stage* opens with a paragraph about Fats, who was top of the bill. It reported,

> There were plenty of friends at the Palladium on Monday to greet Fats Waller, a rhythm pianist from New York on his first visit to London, and it was not long before most at any rate in the audience were enjoying his skilful playing, the humorous expressions on his mobile face and his chuckling observations. Those who like rhythm playing – and their name would appear to be legion at the moment – will find in Fats Waller someone who knows how to provide it in a thoroughly agreeable way.[3]

Other acts on the same bill were the American trio Lowe, Hite, and Stanley (a giant, an average-sized man, and a midget who indulged in amusing antics); the acrobatic dancers Chester Fredericks and Gloria Lane; and Elsie and Doris Waters – already famous for their characters Gert and Daisy, but in this show also contributing "a well arranged turn to show the other sides of their work."

More discerning jazz fans were somewhat disappointed about the support that Waller got from the pit orchestra at the Palladium. Dan Ingman wrote, "At the Palladium he had to rely on the pit orchestra and very little support did he get. Not only was the accompaniment so loud as to drown most of Fats's vocalisms, but it actually dragged one beat behind for a whole chorus until Fats played a miraculous 9-beat break to put it right."[4] Obviously, such comments were beyond the perception of the reviewer for *The Stage* who noticed that Clifford Greenwood and his Orchestra (the pit band) earned cordial applause for their finely played selection from the current hit show *The Fleet's Lit Up*, and "also support the general bill in their customary efficient fashion." It was evident, though, that by the middle of the week the orchestral accompaniment had been cut down and Fats was concentrating on his piano playing, dropping a number in which he played both celesta and piano at the same time.

Reviewers were mixed in their views of Fats's facial mannerisms. *Melody Maker* found the performance to be "of its kind the best we've ever seen on this side of the Atlantic," but sat on the fence on the issue of Fats's mannerisms by asserting that the Palladium was too large for his grimaces and byplay to be seen properly. Nevertheless, he was a sufficient success to be held over for a second week. *The Stage* announced, "Fats Waller remains for a second week and is very popular with his rhythmic playing of current tunes on the pianoforte, adding vocal treatment to some of them, and doing all his work in a cheerful spirit that communicates itself to the audience."[5] The rest of the bill had changed for this second week, and was now headed by the comedian Max Miller. *The Stage* reported,

The programme has characteristically British artists who worthily uphold the home tradition. Mr Miller is a frequent visitor to this house, but he can never come too often for audiences who revel in his cheekiness and good humour as well as in his songs and dances. It is not so much what he does as the way he does it that keeps the audience in laughter, and great is the fun while he holds the stage. This week he brings the *Blackpool Walk* to London and the House is obviously delighted with the number and with his treatment of it.

From being top of the bill the previous week Fats had been relegated to a lower position on the program and it is testament to the power of the variety audience that Max Miller took top billing in preference to a visiting American musician. At the end of his second week at the Palladium, Fats took part in a recording session for HMV on August 21, before opening the following day at the Stratford Empire in East London, where he played two houses a night at 6.30 and 8.50 and was reported thus in *The Stage*: "Fats Waller displays a fine technique at the piano and has a delightful touch. He also sings several American melodies in effective style."[6]

The recording session was the first of two. On August 21 with his "Continental Rhythm" he recorded six sides. A week later, on August 28, he was back in the studio, recording on the Compton organ at HMV's Abbey Road complex, which he also used to accompany the singer Adelaide Hall for two tracks. Jazz enthusiasts were already aware of Adelaide as the singer who had added her wordless vocals to Duke Ellington's 1927 *Creole Love Call*, but she never saw herself as a jazz singer. Rather, she was an extremely accomplished vocalist who had made her reputation in stage shows such as *Shuffle Along* and *Chocolate Kiddies*. By the time she cut her British discs with Waller, she already had a string of successful records to her name. Many of these had been made in London, which was to become her permanent home from the mid-1930s until her death in 1992. Her singing with Fats on *That Old Feeling* is typical of her ability to inject nuance and layers of implied meaning into every line.

A characteristic
"facial
mannerism."

The August 21 session was put together by Fats's manager and the English pianist, composer, and critic Leonard Feather. Feather selected the sidemen for the session, and composed one of the pieces that was recorded: *Don't Try Your Jive on Me.*

The band consisted of the West Indian trumpeter Dave Wilkins, the Scots trombonist George Chisholm, the saxophonists Alfie Cahn and Ian Shepherd (tenor saxophone and violin), the guitarist Alan Ferguson, and the bassist Len Harrison; the drummer on the first track (*Don't Try Your Jive on Me*) was Hymie Schneider, who had been chosen by Feather, but on all the other tracks his place was taken by the young Venezuelan-born percussionist Edmundo Ros, whom Fats had heard playing at various London nightclubs.

The *Sunday Times* critic Iain Lang was at the session. He recalled,

> Nobody at Abbey Road was prepared for the pace at which he
> recorded with hastily assembled musicians who had never
> worked with him, or each other, before. There seemed to be
> only a few minutes' interval between the shouts of "wrap it
> up!" with which Tom signalled approval of each take. Then the
> bottle of John Haig on the piano being empty, we all drifted
> downstairs to listen to him improvise at the console of the
> organ.[7]

The trombonist George Chisholm (later a star on the *Goon Show*), who
interrupted a honeymoon on Jersey to fly back for the session, had
arrived the previous evening and sat in at the Palm Beach Club to get
his lip in shape. George later wrote about the session:

> I always remember while we were making those records he
> used to have a bottle of a well known whisky – John Haig
> actually – on the piano, and he would take a swig every now
> and then. I think he mentions it on one of the records –
> something like "give me some John Haig, man". ... Away
> from work he was just the same happy go lucky kind of guy.
> All fun.

George also recalled that after hours the musicians got together at the
Nest Club, where on one night Fats, Benny Carter, Coleman Hawkins,
and members of the Jimmie Lunceford band all managed to be there at
one time. George sat in with them on one occasion and had a few
wonderful sets.[8]

If George Chisholm had gone to extreme lengths to cut short his
honeymoon and fly back from the Channel Islands, he was rivaled by
the trumpeter Dave Wilkins, who made the journey from Glasgow,
where he had been playing in a show with Snake Hips Johnson on a
kind of reverse of Fats Waller's own itinerary; the Johnson band,
usually resident in London (at the Café de Paris, where they were

The August 21 recording session: (left to right) Ian Shepherd (tenor saxophone and violin); Leonard Feather (producer); Len Harrison (bass); Fats; blurred figure – either Dave Wilkins (trumpet) or Edmundo Ros (drums); Alan Ferguson (guitar); George Chisholm (trombone).

fatally bombed during World War II), were touring for the Moss organization, and had been playing in the very theater in Glasgow at which Fats had appeared a couple of weeks earlier. Wilkins traveled all night in band uniform. He had been asked to get the Saturday night sleeper, since Waller's recording session was to take place on Sunday morning. Although the train journey had taken the average time for those days of ten hours, Wilkins had been so excited at the prospect of recording with his hero that he couldn't sleep on the train. He was met at Euston station and taken by cab to the apartment where Waller was staying, where he was promptly greeted with the words, "I've heard a lot about you. You look as though you could do with a good drink." Fats pointed at the John Haig bottle!

All the other session men gathered at the apartment, and after a couple of glasses of Haig apiece they went by cab to the recording studios.

When Jeff Green talked to Dave Wilkins about the session, he recalled that there was no discussion about what the musicians were to play. They took about thirty minutes for the studio engineers to get a balance, during which time Waller played the piano, joked, and reached for the Haig whisky. Dave Wilkins had previously played neither of the first two tracks to be recorded, *A-Tisket, A-Tasket* and *Pent up in a Penthouse*.

Wilkins thinks he was paid union scale for the recording session, and remembers that afterwards everybody went back to Fats's apartment. Unfortunately, he had to leave early as Johnson's band was to open on Monday at Cardiff in South Wales.[9]

The session produced a rather mixed bag of recordings, and the version of *Ain't Misbehavin'* on which Fats plays the organ with the band is less successful than the versions of *Flat Foot Floogie*, *Pent up in a Penthouse*, *Music Maestro Please*, and *A-Tisket, A-Tasket* on which Fats plays piano. Nevertheless, the sides are of a reasonably high standard given that the European musicians were working with Fats for the first time, and had not had an opportunity to play with him before the recording session.

During the stay in London, Fats was domiciled at a small apartment in St James's, where he was first visited by Iain Lang, among others. Lang remembers Waller, huge in his underwear with a hair net on his head, roaming around the apartment and sending his valet for scotch. Lang was surprised that the name "Fats" was something that Waller really adopted for stage use only. "Anita [his wife], a stickler for social protocol, called him Thomas; his other friends called him Tom." Lang also remembers late-night sessions at the apartment following Waller's concerts at the Holborn and Finsbury Park Empires during the week of August 29.[10]

In early September Waller played in the New Cross Empire in south London and the Kilburn Empire in north-west London. The researcher Howard Rye has conclusively demonstrated that Waller spent the week beginning September 1 in London, rather than in Leeds, as had been suggested by the advertisements in the *Melody Maker* from late August. This is also borne out by the lists of variety performers published every week in *The Stage*, which show Waller on the bill for the London theaters, although unfortunately there appear to be no reviews of his appearance at the Kilburn Empire.[11]

On September 11, Fats Waller left Harwich for Holland, *en route* for Scandinavia. He stayed there until the very end of September, arriving back in England on the 28th. He was most impressed with audiences in Scandinavia, and we can discern a distinct difference in the attitude of European audiences from those Fats was more used to in the United States from his comments in a November 1938 interview with the *World Telegram*. He said,

> Throughout the British Isles and Scandinavia, audiences like to listen ... Unlike the jitterbugs over here, they will often stop while dancing as a band builds up to the climaxes. I never saw such an intelligent appreciation of swing. After one concert I gave in Sweden a chap came up to me and said "what did you play in that 17th bar of the 4th chorus?" He killed me, but it's typical of the response you get.

On September 29, it is evident that Fats broadcast for the BBC, although the time scheduled in the *Radio Times* was apparently changed owing to certain political events going on in Munich at the same time and he appeared at 5.00 pm, some four hours earlier than advertised. Fats's television appearance was made on September 30, and photographs of this broadcast exist. However, the published schedule listings in the *Radio Times* were again changed at short notice, and Waller appeared unbilled at 9.00 pm that evening.

On October 1, 1938, Fats returned to New York. The English visit had been a great success. Fats had made a distinguished mark on the variety circuit, holding his own against native British performers of great popularity, and he had also made two valuable series of recordings. On the second date, August 28, he had recorded some excellent organ solos of Negro spirituals in addition to the sides with Adelaide Hall. Although there are some recording problems with the organ, and its full dynamic range isn't readily apparent from the recordings, nevertheless these are some of Waller's finest performances on the pipe organ.

It was not, however, until the following year – 1939 – that Fats realized his most successful recording project in Europe, when he recorded his *London Suite* for HMV (after having made a privately recorded test version of it, which is now lost, earlier in his visit to England the same year). The *London Suite* is discussed more fully in Chapter 7, and is one of the most remarkable sustained pieces of solo piano work that Fats committed to disc. It shows that in 1939 he was at the very peak of his creative form on keyboard.

In 1939, unlike his previous visit, Fats arrived on the *Queen Mary*. Docking in Southampton on March 16 he moved to London where on the 20th he opened at the Holborn Empire. This time he doubled with the Mills Brothers, appearing both at Holborn and at Finsbury Park. His protégée Una Mae Carlisle was in hospital at the time and she received an unexpected visit from Fats on the 26th.

Once again Fats toured the variety circuit, and between March 27 and the end of June he appeared in Croydon, Birmingham, Glasgow, Sunderland, Edinburgh, Portsmouth, Brighton, Nottingham, Sheffield, Manchester, and Newcastle.

At Brighton, on the evening of Monday May 8, Fats went across after his show at the Hippodrome to Sherry's (where he had played a cabaret engagement the previous year) to hear Nat Gonella and his band. The English critic Jeff Atterton was at Sherry's for the 1938 cabaret engagement. He recalled,

> The place was packed to capacity and the most important thing to me was getting as close as possible to that white grand piano ... Fats, a resplendent figure in black satin jacket and grey pants, made his appearance through the tables to a tremendous roar of applause from a large crowd of dancers and spectators who had gathered to welcome him. Sherry's was the first ballroom Waller had visited in Europe and no man could have wished for a warmer reception.[12]

Fats on stage
during his 1939
tour of the Moss
Empires circuit.

Indeed, in 1938, Gonella had been playing in the same town, only
that year it was Gonella who was at the Hippodrome. In 1939, the
locations reversed: Fats dropped into Sherry's to hear Nat, and,
according to Gonella's biographer Ron Brown, "over a bottle of gin he
was persuaded to sit in on a jam session."[13] Gonella recalled that the
management at the Hippodrome were not amused, taking a dim view of
their star playing somewhere else for free, so they fined Fats £50 for
breaking his contract. Apparently Waller was extremely cross, and felt
that for the cost of a couple of cases of gin he should leave the tour then
and there and return to the USA. Fortunately, Ed Kirkeby's persuasive
powers won the day and he remained in England to finish his tour.

Once more the press was split in its view about Fats's performances. Nearly all the papers concentrated on Fats's facial and

Nat Gonella.

vocal antics at the expense of his piano playing. Nevertheless, he made many friends in Europe, and confirmed the popularity that his recordings had already created for him to some extent by coming to Europe in person. He has remained much loved in Europe ever since, and the oft-quoted *Melody Maker* farewell tribute is entirely appropriate. When Fats returned to America for the last time on June 14, 1939, *Melody Maker* said: "One of the most brilliant true jazz artists ever to come from America to Britain, he returns a more popular idol than ever, and will long be remembered with great affection."

THE FINAL YEARS

B y 1940, the stages of Waller's life had fallen relatively neatly into the rags-to-riches pattern. He had grown up in, and never lost touch with, the Harlem community. He had become a celebrated pianist and organist. He had performed in vaudeville. He had written scores of hit songs and at least two major Broadway shows. He had performed on radio and in the movies, and was the leader of an extremely popular recording band. He had toured Europe with considerable success. His contemporaries remember that while he had not completely extricated himself from his financial problems concerned with his first marriage, he was nevertheless earning substantial amounts of money. Like James P. Johnson, he had moved out of Manhattan into Queens.

Yet if there is one thing that all those who knew him are agreed about, it was that Thomas Waller was an unfulfilled man. He would take people out to his house and play the classics, or his own more serious compositions, for hours. His sidemen, friends, and overseas visitors all remarked that he became increasingly disenchanted with the crass songs he was required to record (often, it seems, because nobody else was likely to make a commercial success of the numbers). He was, as we know from Gene Sedric, equally unhappy that his club and theater audiences would sit silently through his more measured and sophisticated performances until someone would shout a request for him to "swing it," and the old routines would emerge.

The *London Suite* is a pointer to the direction in which his interests lay, but compared with the emergent talent of Art Tatum, it shows something of the limitations of Waller's keyboard approach from that of the men who were the up and coming generation of jazzmen. Some critics have pointed out the incongruity of Fats continuing the 1920s rent party stride piano style through into the swing era, and many listeners have found the conflict between his dazzling keyboard style (and ability to swing) and his self-image as an "entertainer" a barrier to appreciating his work fully. Natural innocent that Fats might have been in some respects, he was too good and too sensitive a musician for the issues to pass him by altogether.

He fostered the story of his classical tuition. He fueled rumors about playing the organ at Notre Dame. He endorsed in words (if not entirely in deeds) the received values of James P. Johnson: "Next to a grand organ there's nothing finer than a magnificent symphony orchestra. I get my kicks out of that kind of music as well as spontaneous jazz."[1] All these remarks affirm his sense of isolation and lack of fulfillment. He was beginning to work with Ed Kirkeby to change his career pattern – to spend more time at home with his family, with the leisure to compose, to study the classics. He turned again to show composition with *Early to Bed*, and in 1943 he also made his most successful film appearance in *Stormy Weather*. But sadly the planned change in Waller's life was not to be.

Despite his intentions to make a change of direction in his career, the period that began with Fats's return from Europe until the point he broke up his big band in May 1943 was one of relentless touring, club, and concert appearances, plus continued recording activity. The last few months of 1939, for instance, saw Waller hastily assemble a new band within a week of landing back in New York, with replacements for Al Casey, Gene Sedric, and Slick Jones, who had taken other jobs during his European tour. In just over a week, this line-up was in the studio for Victor, before it went on to play a week at the Apollo, followed by an appearance at the World's Fair in Manhattan, and a long road tour. There were more solo and band recordings for a transcription service, another Victor session with Sedric and Jones back in the fold, several weeks of gigs in Chicago, a week in Boston, a visit to New Haven, and a residency at the Famous Door, as the band came home at last to New York. No sooner had the band closed at the club than it was back at the Apollo with a further Victor record date to be squeezed in. By the year end, Fats had also held down residencies in Pittsburgh, Washington, and – once again – Chicago, not to mention being sued for non-appearance by a club owner in Millsboro, Delaware.[2]

This pressure of work, coupled with Fats's hedonistic lifestyle, was bound to take its toll, and matters did not improve when his newly assembled big band began notching up a colossal mileage in the first half of 1940, with seasons in Florida and then a national tour. Some of the bookings on this tour were far from urban, smooth, and professional. Trumpeter Franc Williams remembered one gig where the road petered out some miles from the settlement where they were due to perform, and the musicians and instruments being transported the last few miles on horseback.[3] A number of sidemen were so exhausted by the tour that they decided to leave, including saxophonist Franz Jackson, who told me:

> I left Fats to join Earl Hines, because instead of touring, he was based in one place in my home town of Chicago. I joined him on the closure of that national tour with Fats, which had been a really dissipating experience. From his lifestyle and the general messy organization, I was tired out. We'd worked our way back from L. A. through the mountains, playing a lot of deadhead gigs, many of which really didn't work out. So when we stopped off at Union Station in Chicago to put Fats on the train home to New York, I pulled my bag off the bus there and then and left the band at the same time.[4]

There were signs that Fats's health had been breaking down since his return from Europe in 1939, and this hectic rate of work coupled with Fats's predilection for partying accelerated the process. His sidemen (such as Herb Flemming, in the story quoted in Chapter 3) recall his swollen limbs, his pain while walking, and his propensity for minor infections. Fats's great resilience and strength made light of most of these, but he grew tired easily, and his resistance to touring continued. His indulgence in food and alcohol went on unabated, and the long-term effects on his system must have been damaging. He still weighed about 285 pounds. It is remarkable how little his alcoholic intake seems to have affected his playing, and his coordination was almost always exceptional.

During his second trip in 1943 to the West Coast, he developed a severe bronchial condition while playing at the Club Zanzibar. According to Ed Kirkeby, Fats had to play, pouring with sweat, under an air-conditioning fan that gave him first a chill, then 'flu, then bronchitis. He was confined to bed for ten days under doctor's orders, but returned to the club to finish the engagement, apparently recovered, but still near the chilling blast of the fan.

At the end of the engagement, there was the usual round of all-night parties, and on the morning of December 13, Kirkeby and Waller set out for the Santa Fe Chief, which left at noon for the long journey (it took several days) to New York. The party of well-wishers at the station included the drummer Tommy Benford (who was in California with Noble Sissle), the trumpeters Wendell Culley and Demus Dean, and (according to his biographer Hans Mückenberger) Jack Teagarden. Another party of fans joined Fats in the club car of the train for a celebration in anticipation of the return to the East.

Exhausted, Waller slept all day on the 14th. During the small hours of the morning of the 15th, Kirkeby entered their berth as the train swept across the Kansas plains. It was bitterly cold, and Fats woke briefly to joke that the gusty wind sounded like the tenor sax of Coleman Hawkins.

At five in the morning, as the train pulled into Kansas Union

Station, Kirkeby was woken by the sound of Fats shivering in the neighboring berth. As Fats gasped for breath, his manager went for help. Kirkeby found a doctor: "I told him Fats was very sick and hurried him to our car. The doctor took one look. 'This man is dead,' he said."[5]

By coincidence, the bassist Gene Ramey was working on the station that night. Another railwayman told him a "fellow musician" had died on the train. It was not until later that Ramey discovered it had been Fats. Like everyone, everywhere, who ever knew Fats, or even heard and enjoyed one of his records, he felt a deep and lasting sense of loss.[6]

The funeral was a large affair, packed with friends, fans, and the people of Harlem. Adam Clayton Powell made a speech in memory of his old family friend.

With the passing of Fats Waller, the world lost a man who brought much happiness to many people. This book has been an attempt to sum up his life and times, and to clarify some of the stories and some of the facts that surrounded Fats. But to summarize the whole thing, it is most appropriate to use the words of Dick Wellstood, who died suddenly in the summer of 1987, but who, as a younger generation stride pianist, was one of the keepers of the flame.

> The rags, cotillions, mazurkas and all those other unknown phenomena all came together in James P., who made jazz out of them, and then the harmonies of James P. went into Duke, the showiness into Tatum, the goodtiminess into Fats and the rhythmic potentialities into Monk ... and Basie stole the skeleton.
>
> [Fats] plays a goodtime version of James P. James P. plays the full tune. Fats abstracts what he wants from it. He plays half the tune in effect. *His* half.[7]

THE RECORDS

F ats Waller's recorded output is considerable, given that he died relatively early and did not survive into the LP era. We are lucky enough to have some extended examples of his playing (notably from the transcriptions of his broadcasts that have been preserved), but the vast majority of his output is in the form of 78 rpm recordings, each item limited by the form of the ten-inch disc to a playing time of three and a half minutes. (Unusually for a jazzman, Fats was privileged to be allowed a 12-inch 78 for the instrumental versions of *Honeysuckle Rose* and *Blue Turning Grey* which came out back-to-back on Victor 36206.)

The most comprehensive survey of Waller's recordings is Laurie Wright's book *Fats in Fact*, with Howard Rye's comprehensive companion volume listing microgroove reissues. In this chapter I have followed Wright's practice of identifying each performance by the number of the original 78 rpm issue. Because the body of recordings is so large, it is divided into five sections: the piano solos, the organ solos, work with other bands, the Rhythm (and Continental Rhythm), and the big bands. In each, there is a critical overview, and an attempt to pick out particularly important or significant recordings, to focus on the most worthwhile of Waller's numerous recordings, and to try to unearth the musical gems from over-commercial, satirical, or silly performances.

For anyone wishing to assemble a collection of Fats Waller records, there are comprehensive editions on the French Classics label, and a relatively complete coverage on RCA Bluebird CDs. The six double albums on the French RCA's Jazz Tribune label have also made occasional appearances on CD. The most thorough collection issued is still the French RCA "Complete Recordings" series on LP, produced in the 1970s and 1980s.

THE PIANO SOLOS

Waller's solo piano works (as composer and performer) have attracted more critical attention than any other part of his output – although Morroe Berger's pioneering study of Waller's vocal style and Paul Machlin's book on all aspects of Waller's music have opened up some new areas for discussion. Max Harrison's analysis of Waller's early piano work in *Jazz Monthly* (December 1965, reprinted in his book *A Jazz Retrospect*) rightly takes the view that the peak of Waller's early creativity was reached in the series of piano solos he recorded in 1929. Remarkably (at least at first glance), the central group of these was recorded in just one session – on August 2, 1929. Eleven takes of six different pieces included definitive piano versions of *Ain't Misbehavin'* (Victor 22092), *Sweet Savannah Sue* (Victor 22108), *I've Got a Feeling I'm Falling* (Victor 22092), and *Valentine Stomp* (Victor V38554).

But considering what we know of Waller's studio and broadcasting technique, it is not surprising to find him reeling off a string of polished performances on record in just the way he might in a club or on the air. In 1929, he was at his creative peak, with *Hot Chocolates* running on Broadway and at Connie's, and by comparing take with take from the 1929 record dates we find him adjusting, refining, and adapting his performances (as well as, occasionally, losing his way and skillfully covering this up) in a way that reinforces Mezzrow's view of the

Connie's rehearsals, and which ties in with Razaf's memory of Fats's perfectionism. In looking at all of his piano output in a similar way, it is possible to observe its high points as being other moments where he had the opportunity to extend his ideas at leisure, such as in the famous *London Suite*.

In surveying Waller's piano output as an entity, it is preferable to ignore the 1922 phonograph recordings of *Muscle Shoals Blues* and *Birmingham Blues* in favor of the first group of piano rolls from 1923. We know from Michael Montgomery's research that Fats would practice for a couple of hours or so before recording a performance onto a master roll from which the commercial versions would be produced. Hence the final versions of each of his rolls could be seen as the culmination of a similar contemplative period at the keyboard to that which was recorded in full in the August 1929 Victor session. The playing on *Got to Cool My Doggies Now*, his first roll, is not exceptional, except that it demonstrates how (even in 1923) Fats had mastered the idea of "backward tenths," in which the left hand strikes intervals of a

Contemporary caricature of Fats by Milos, widely used in his publicity and sheet music.

tenth on the first and third beats of each bar at fractionally different times, the little finger carrying a strong bass line, while the thumb (playing the upper note) sets up what is in effect a counter melody to the tune. The author has watched the hands of such accomplished disciples of Fats as Ralph Sutton and Don Ewell as they replicate this effect: Ewell in particular could emulate Fats well, keeping the oompah stride beat moving forward effortlessly and ornamenting the melody with his right hand, yet interpolating a distinctive internal melodic line.

All Waller's surviving piano roll output is preserved on three Biograph LPs, recorded in the early 1970s by Michael Montgomery on a 1910 Steinway Upright player piano. The LPs include rolls of tunes written by Waller, but not necessarily played by him, as well as his own performances. Highlights of the performances by Waller include his measured version of *Your Time Now* from May 1923, which includes descending bell-like figures and other complex effects in the main tune, as well as a series of devices for breaking the pattern of the left-hand rhythms, such as ascending chromatic figures and odd two-bar fragments of boogie-woogie; the piece then breaks into a final hell-for-leather sixteen bars which is pure stride, the right hand taking a plummeting line from patterns played at the very upper limit of the keyboard. *Tain't Nobody's Bizness*, released in June 1923, has some startlingly effective right-hand patterns in the second chorus and some passages of splendid playing. Nothing else in the set of Waller's own performances is quite so splendid, however, as *A New Kind of Man*, made in 1924 for QRS's rival company Standard, on which Waller plays a staggeringly difficult set piece in the third chorus, changing the triad chord in the left hand on every beat.

The high point of all three Biograph albums, however, is the version of *If I Could Be with You* (James P. Johnson's 1926 song) recorded by Waller and Johnson together on two pianos jointly connected to the master recording machine. This is a performance which (despite the slightly rigid nature of all player-piano reproductions) gives a genuine sense of the excitement that the master and pupil team could create. (The three albums are Biograph 1002Q, 1005Q, and 1015Q.)

At the third session of Waller's Victor contract (February 1927), after making his obligatory organ solos, he cut a piano solo version of the *Blue Black Bottom* (not originally issued on 78). This represents his first solo piano recording in a non-accompanimental role since his great period of activity for QRS piano rolls in 1923–4. He also seems to have cut three versions of *Black Bottom Is the Latest Fad*, but none has been issued. The *Blue Black Bottom* begins rather shakily, and after a chorus of left-hand melody the tempo gradually accelerates as Waller picks up the full two-fisted stride version of this tune he had written with Mike Jackson for publication by Ralph Peer. It is not a particularly good or memorable performance, but it shows, especially in its uneven tempo, that Fats had lessons to learn in the transition from recording via piano roll to making gramophone records, where the speed of the performance could not be varied in the same way by the operator of the equipment. The track is included on the French RCA five-album Memorial Set, Vol. 1, RCA 730 570.

By 1929, when Waller began the recording of his great series of piano solos, there were no such problems. *Numb Fumblin'* and *Handful of Keys* (both Victor V38508) were cut at the same notorious session as the band tracks recalled by Eddie Condon, *Minor Drag* and *Harlem Fuss*. They could hardly be more different, either from each other, or from the band performances. *Numb Fumblin'* is a gentle, slowish piece, and although it is a twelve-bar blues, in many respects it is much more like one of the pieces of the then fashionable school of "novelty" piano than many more out-and-out blues performances. It is redolent of a strain of contemplative, self-consciously "pretty" music for which Johnson and Willie "the Lion" as well as Waller had a propensity. In the Lion's great series of solo recordings made for Milt Gabler's Commodore label in 1939 (reissued on Commodore Classics 6.25491) there is a great deal in this vein; indeed, the Lion's famous *Echoes of Spring* typifies it.

Numb Fumblin' builds from a gentle introduction into a succession of choruses, each of which develops the idea a little further, culminating in a dazzling sequence of high treble figures in the right hand. The development in each chorus is based on stride motifs rather than the clichés of piano blues, and while some critics (Max Harrison and Dick Wellstood among them) have seen this as "showbiz" blues playing, they miss the point that this kind of pianistic "novelty" blues (swinging nonetheless) is part of the common vocabulary of the great stride players.

But if proof were needed that in 1929 Fats had joined the ranks of those great exponents of stride, one need look no further than

Fats (with the bandleader Billy Higgs) poses for the camera before one of his radio broadcasts.

Handful of Keys. For generations of pianists, this piece came to represent one of the great set pieces, alongside Johnson's *Carolina Shout.* The 1929 recording is masterly, setting out as it does the successive strains in the manner of a ragtime composition: every note of the performance sounds right – at the same time composed, yet spontaneous, and with the underlying sense (inherent in the title) that it is a very "pianistic" number. This is obvious from the outset, as the first theme uses an upward scale as its main motif, which is repeated an octave higher on the second chorus. The bridge passages lead to two further main themes, then a series of broken chords (another device from the piano exercise books) leads into the final part of the last chorus, where repeated right-hand chords act rather like a big-band riff against the inexorable progress of the left hand. Much of the piece, both in its structure, and in the devices of the last chorus, is reminiscent of the multi-thematic compositions of Jelly Roll Morton.

Later in his career, Waller took to playing the number as a solo feature in concerts and on club dates. We are fortunate that a recording survives of a broadcast from the NBC studios (May 7, 1938; GOJ 1041) in which he featured *Handful of Keys.* Here he takes the tune much faster than on the 1929 version, and with a finesse that shows his keyboard prowess had developed in the intervening nine years. He almost parodies his younger self (especially in the way he uses the first theme as the basis for the bridge passage to the final section), but again the composition works as a stride set piece, and Waller performs it with consummate skill. Two other versions of the tune survive, both from radio transcriptions made shortly before Fats's death in 1943. Both suffer to some extent from Waller's view of himself as a show business personality. One is from the "Charlie McCarthy Show," and sits uneasily between jokes about Fats's girth ("Turn around Fats, so we can see how the other half lives"). The second is from the "AFRS Command Performance." The tune is anyway an odd choice for a two-number spot in a wartime radio request program, but it suffers here from following a characteristically jokey performance of *Your Feet's Too Big.* Fats quells the applause for the comic song with shouts of "Cease!", and launches at breakneck speed into *Handful of Keys*.

Once again, the piano technique is remarkable, with Fats's usual clarity of touch and delicate variations in dynamics. But soon he starts to shout a commentary at the studio audience. Here his "I wonder what the poor people are doing tonight?" is played for laughs, and bears little resemblance to the tone of social comment in which he first used the remark. Moving on from this ill-judged joke, he abruptly stops his performance two bars from the end of a chorus, shouts, "Come out of there!", and, to shrieks from the audience, picks up the tune at the end of the two-bar break. As if palpitating from the suspense of wondering if he will be able to pick up the performance on cue, he shouts, "Be still, my heart, be still!", to roars from the audience. It is here that the performance almost breaks down. He muffs the first of the broken chords entirely, and once more (though with an irony obvious to those who know the tune) he shouts, "Come on out of there", pulls himself through, and finishes the home straight at great speed amid shouts of "How 'bout that?"

This comparison illuminates very clearly the difference between the young Waller, at twenty-five and at the height of his creative energy, setting out a near-perfect version of his own classic stride composition (albeit after a night on the town and following a recording made with a hastily assembled pick-up band), and the thirty-nine-year-old popular entertainer concealing even greater keyboard technique with a veneer of patter and jokes, which, in the final example, stray into his playing itself. This, more than anything, displays the point made by Dick Wellstood in the *Jazz Review*, when he told Martin Williams,

> It's so hard to tell what Fats could do, because he was always trying to entertain, and so made his playing entertaining at the damndest times ... the trouble with a lot of those guys of that age is they really in a sense are ashamed of jazz, and sometimes you have to force them to play good.

There are one or two other surviving solo versions of *Handful of Keys*, but rather than dwell on these, we should return to 1929 and to the magnificent set of solos recorded between August 2 and September 24. These are all included in RCA's double CD set of Waller's complete Victor/Bluebird piano recordings 1929–1941 (RCA ND 89741). The bulk of the first two sessions (August 2 and 29) are also to be found on the French RCA *Complete Recordings* Vols. 3 and 4 (741 076 and 741 086). None of the pieces here is of quite the same stature as *Handful of Keys*, although *Gladyse* (Victor V38554) and *Valentine Stomp* (also V38554) are both major contributions to stride piano. Paul Machlin and Max Harrison, as well as Humphrey Lyttelton (in an entertaining piece in *The Best of Jazz Vol. 2*), have written at length about these performances, noting everything from their construction to variations in individual versions and passages that crop up in more than one number. The important point is that the August 2 session consisted of an extended series of piano improvisations, allowing Fats to develop his ideas at length. There has to be an exception to every rule, however, and on September 24, 1929, Fats recorded just one piece. Like *Handful of Keys*, *Smashing Thirds* (Victor V38613) turned out to be one of his masterpieces.

Once again, Waller uses devices from the piano exercise book as an integral part of his composition. The third chorus involves upward moving scales played in harmony; the sixth and seventh have a downward moving left-hand figure which is sporadically interrupted, drawing the listener's attention to it on each occasion. *Smashing Thirds* is a somewhat more subtle piece than *Handful of Keys*, and something less of a bravura showpiece. It was not a composition that Waller played regularly in subsequent radio or Muzak transcription recordings.

Apart from a couple of solos recorded in December 1929 (*My Fate Is in Your Hands* and *Turn On the Heat*, both Victor V38568), and two rather good piano duets recorded in March 1930 with Cab Calloway's pianist Bennie Payne, the next significant set of Waller's piano solos dates from November 16, 1934. On that day Fats recorded four remarkable sides, each one a classic, and each employing a contrast of styles between different sections of the piece. *African Ripples* (Victor 24830) begins and ends with an up-tempo stride motif (the "ripples" of the title) which is familiar from *Gladyse* of 1929. There is a slower, reflective central section that leads after four choruses or so into a stately theme; this concludes with a bravura bridge passage, with plenty of ideas borrowed from classical piano cadenzas, and is followed by a furious restatement of the opening theme. The playing shows a range of variation in touch and feeling which was only beginning to

Promotion flyer for the sheet music series in which Fats's November 1934 recordings were published.

emerge in 1929, and we could reasonably expect this to be the kind of piece that Fats would perform at the Riverside Drive parties where he mingled with Gershwin and Godowsky.

Alligator Crawl, most uncharacteristically for Waller (who in later life used to insert a clause in his contracts saying he would not play boogie-woogie), is built around a rolling left-hand boogie figure, while *Viper's Drag* (Victor 25015) sets a couple of choruses of unbridled stride in the context of a slower left-hand ostinato figure against rolling right-hand tremolos. If each of these pieces places contrasting sections in apposition to one another, *Clothes Line Ballet* (issued on the reverse of *Viper's Drag*) makes use of a series of much shorter comparisons, four slow bars being followed by four fast ones, before the main 32-bar theme is introduced; this is followed in turn by yet more contrasting four-bar units.

In these four pieces there is a sense of overall unity of thought and ideas, and they sound more thoroughly worked out than some of the lesser 1929 recordings, which are either window-dressed conventional 32-bar themes, or sections of stride motifs stitched together in a new order. They were published as a set (in a series of "Rhythmic Piano Solos" by various composers), and Waller recorded all of them again in his March 1935 series of 16-inch transcription discs for the Muzak company. All the recorded versions of the tunes are sophisticated improvements over the published form of the music – Waller's ability to recompose passages as he went (either from lapse of memory or as spur-of-the-moment alterations) giving us a further chance to examine his creative process, and his formidable technique allowing us to spot the places where he could outstretch the hands of lesser pianists. (The transcription discs have been issued several times, including the French RCA's Black and White series Vols. 21 and 22, 730 659 and 730 660. It was of these that Hugues Panassié wrote: "these discs are the only ones which fully recapture for me his true vocal timbre, with both the warmth and tenderness which habitually fail to be brought to life for us on disc."[1])

The transcription discs once more illustrate how Fats was at his best playing over a period of some hours and being recorded the while. On March 11, 1935, he cut no fewer than sixteen masters, the last eight being medleys of three tunes apiece.

The best sustained example of his piano work, however, is the *London Suite* (HMV B10059, 10060, 10061) cut on June 13, 1939 in London. The surviving issued versions are dubbed from test pressings, since the original masters were destroyed during World War II.

Only one of these pieces is an up-tempo stride showstopper, and this is *Piccadilly*, which borrows one of its themes from *Valentine Stomp*. All the others are medium or slow in pace, and tread a narrow line between being as inconsequential as cocktail-bar music on the one hand and sending up the light classics on the other, while not failing to remain jazz performances. *Chelsea*, for instance, has an out-of-tempo restatement of its theme at the end, the piece being concluded by a showy cadenza; somehow Fats manages to bring this off within the bounds of good taste. Starting *Soho*, he picks up the contour of the theme of *Chelsea* in his introduction, before starting to develop a new melody built out of short repeated figures. The compositional technique is not particularly original, and he had used the same methods in many of his other piano works; here, however, there is a grace about his playing that marks out the performance as unusual, despite the obvious limitations of recording quality that result from the use of a test pressing as source material.

The other three pieces are also interesting. While the tempos are all similar, Waller manages to surprise the listener by some very original turns of thought. *Bond Street* has another melody built of a repeated phrase, but here the phrase is repeated three times over the eight main bars of the melodic structure, the last two bars of the eight serving the same function as a two-bar break in a Harlem jive riff tune. The piece works well within the 32-bar structure, the starting point of the second 32 bars being pitched surprisingly, and sounding like a reprise of the middle eight. In *Limehouse* the effects are oriental, with liberal use of the pentatonic scale both in the introduction and at the end of each section of the main melody. There is a sense of "Chinatown" cliché here, but once more Waller remains tasteful. *Whitechapel*, the final piece, avoids classical pastiche by a whisker. It sounds a bit like one of Art Tatum's developments of a classical theme, except that no classical theme emerges; Waller merely plays dignified opening chords and a grand statement of his own melody, with quotes from the classics here and there, including the *Peer Gynt* suite.

Mention of Tatum (who acknowledged Waller as the source of much of his style) brings us to two sessions in late 1939 (after Waller's return from Europe) at which Fats cut sides that offer the opportunity to compare him with Tatum.

On August 7, less than a month after the London recordings, he took part in a session for Muzak at which a fairly awful solo version of *Handful of Keys* was cut, along with a tune Fats had recorded in London but which HMV rejected. This was *Hallelujah*, which Waller often used on his broadcasts (versions exist on the GOJ reissues of his radio shots), and which was recorded by Tatum in a spectacular solo version (issued on Black Lion 2460 158 from a 1945 Los Angeles session). While Tatum paraphrases the melody in a straight run-through of the tune, before one faster stride chorus, then an even faster, dazzling final chorus replete with his effortless runs in both hands, Waller begins with stentorian opening chords and plays a corny statement of the tune in the high treble with some conventional stride patterns, before some crashing final chords and a ghostly half statement of the theme in the upper register. There is no doubt that Tatum's is the more forward-looking, jazzier performance of the two, while Fats contrasts Tatum's effortless evenness of touch with far more dynamic variety and conscious exploitation of the extremes of the keyboard.

Another comparison is offered by the Lang-Worth transcription discs which Waller recorded at the end of 1939, and on which he produced gently "swung" versions of the classics – a rather banal four-to-the-bar rendition of the waltz from Gounod's *Faust*, and the "Intermezzo" from *Cavalleria Rusticana*. Compared with Tatum's versions of Massenet's *Elégie* or Dvořák's *Humoresque*, Waller's attempts sound dated. What is far more interesting is the extent to which Waller brought his appreciation of classical piano technique to bear on his jazz solo playing, which is ultimately a far more fruitful cross-fertilization than an attempt to "swing" the classics. How far he was able to take this is apparent in the last great set of piano solos he recorded, on May 13, 1941.

If Fats the solo pianist had consciously tried to sum up his career in one session he could hardly have done better than this (all of which is preserved on the French RCA *Complete Recordings* Vol. 22, PM 43296). His debt to James P. Johnson is amply repaid in two excellent takes of *Carolina Shout*. He displays his affinity for the classics in the curious *Honeysuckle Rose* (à la Bach, Beethoven, Brahms and Waller) and on *Georgia* he uses a long introduction as a route into some glorious choruses of stride. His version of Ellington's *Ring dem Bells* is as forward looking as anything he ever recorded. As from the earliest days, this session (which also produced a solo version of *Rockin' Chair* and four band tracks) shows how, in the right mood, Fats used long periods of studio time very creatively, benefitting as always from the time to let his ideas as a soloist flow.

THE ORGAN SOLOS

In any consideration of Fats Waller's organ playing it is as well to realize from the outset first that the instrument is formidably difficult to use for successful jazz performance, and second that a man whose penchant for organ playing was fueled initially by Harlem church-going, and subsequently by the jobs of cinema organist and anonymous host of radio WLW's "Moon River," might not have jazz performances uppermost in his mind when sitting at the organ console. There is no doubt he used the pipe organ as a vehicle for improvisation, and that some of this is very impressive, but those who expect the swinging drive of Waller's piano work in his organ recordings may find them disappointing. It was not until the late

1930s, when Fats started recording regularly on the Hammond organ, with its great percussive qualities and the absence of the time delays which were integral to the church or concert organ, that we can begin to hear the genuine jazz possibilities of the instrument in Fats's hands.

Fats's solo organ recordings fall neatly into four groups: the pipe organ recordings made at Camden (1926–9), the pipe organ recordings made for HMV in London (1938, 1939), the Hammond organ transcription discs (1939), and final solos for V-disc (1943). He also used the instrument with a number of bands, including those of Thomas Morris and Fletcher Henderson, as well as the Louisiana Sugar Babes.

The late 1920s sides, produced at the behest of Nat Shilkret and Ralph Peer, have been very fully discussed by Paul Machlin in *Stride*, and he draws attention to *Rusty Pail* (1927, Victor 20492 and a second take), and to *I Ain't Got Nobody* (1927, Victor 21127) in particular. The first (given the opportunity to compare takes) is a good example of Waller's use of changes in registration, while the second gives a fair impression of his probable cinema style. The bulk of Fats's output from this period can be found on the first two volumes of the French RCA's complete reissue (741 052 and 741 062).

Far less critical attention has been lavished on the 1938 and 1939 London recordings. The core of these is a group of solos based on Negro spirituals. One, *Water Boy* (HMV B8845), can be disregarded fairly promptly, in that it suffers from both poor recording balance and choice of registration, so that Waller's attempts to swing give it the sound of a steam launch, or of Fate Marable's calliope atop the Mississippi steamers of the Streckfus line.

Swing Low, Sweet Chariot (HMV B8818) is a very different matter. The performance begins with a rapid figure, which would not be out of place in a Bach toccata, repeated over and over, against which, in a middle register, Fats hints at the tune. He then plays the verse on full organ, using (until the last bar) conventional gospel church harmonies. After a re-harmonized last bar, he starts to swing

"I looked over Jordan" with a heavy on-beat, but after a bar or two, thinks better of it, and begins a routine of question and answer phrases, keeping a semblance of a stride beat going with the pedals. It is a splendid performance, lacking neither in religious feeling and dignity nor in jazz sensibility.

A similar sense comes across in *Go Down, Moses* and *Deep River* (both HMV B8816). In the former, after an impressive introduction, Waller uses a choice of harsh-sounding stops and the swell (or volume) pedal to add an emotional intensity to the first statement of the theme. The rhythmic treatment of the second chorus owes much to the feeling of a gospel choir, and the performance ends with an upwardly spiraling bass figure leading into a final run through the theme, which pulls back the tempo slightly and adds dignity and power to the already apparent sense of religious passion. Here, and in *Deep River*, the pace of Waller's performances and the choice of tempo and registration are masterly, and on these two recordings alone it is possible to see how he acquired his great reputation as an organist.

His Hammond organ work is to some extent marred. First, his 1939 sides are all accompaniments to his own singing, and second, while they show the facility with which Fats had adapted his technique to the electric instrument, there are too few choruses on which we can hear what he was capable of. Fortunately, we can make a direct comparison with vocal versions of *Go Down, Moses* and *Swing Low* (which has been reissued on Deluxe DE 601) and the London recordings, where, despite some similarities in keyboard approach, the Hammond versions have none of the same intensity or feeling. They do show Fats's ability to get a sharply rhythmic performance out of the electric instrument and also the much more abrupt changes in volume afforded by the swell pedal.

On the last two, rather sad, recordings from 1943, inebriation prevented Fats from giving of his best, and *In My Solitude* (V-Disc V658A) and *Sometimes I Feel Like a Motherless Child* (V743A) are best gently forgotten. (Both appear on the French RCA's supplementary album to their complete reissue, 731 058.) Here, changes of register, fumbled fingering, and alarming volume changes do nothing to recall the passion and power of the London spirituals.

WITH OTHER BANDS

Waller recorded with a number of bands under the direction of other leaders both before and during the period of his recordings with the Rhythm. The best of these (and some of the bands under his own leadership which precede the Rhythm) are discussed here.

Fats's first significant partnership with another bandleader came in 1926 with his first two dates with Fletcher Henderson; the band recorded *Henderson Stomp* and Mel Stitzel's *The Chant* (both Columbia 817D) on November 3. Don Redman's arrangement of *The Chant* is pedestrian by comparison with Morton's famous Red Hot Peppers version of a couple of months before. Fats plays the organ in place of piano, and this contributes to the general lack of movement. He plays organ chords in the introduction and harmonies behind Charlie Dixon's banjo solo and at the end of the piece; otherwise it is hard to hear the instrument and it muddies the sound somewhat.

Far more successful are Fats's contributions to *Whiteman Stomp* and *I'm Coming Virginia* which he cut with Henderson in May 1927. On the former there is no piano solo chorus as such, but Fats plays some attractive solo breaks. The first group of these, because of the sheer complexity of the rhythmic line, has the effect of appearing to delay the performance slightly, while the second prefigures an upward moving motif subsequently adopted by the reeds and brass. It's clear that Fats is simply playing Redman's arrangement, and not contributing original piano ideas of his own. The number would not have sounded very different with Henderson himself at the piano. But this could not be said of *I'm Coming Virginia*, where towards the beginning Fats contributes an elegant chorus of his own (in accompaniment to a muted trumpet statement of the theme) before a really excellent trumpet solo from Joe Smith. (Henderson's entire output for Columbia was remastered and reissued on VJM, and most of Waller's tracks are on Vol. 3, VLP 42.)

The next significant collaboration is to be found on the 1927 sides with Thomas Morris. The first of these, *Fats Waller Stomp* (Victor 20890), marks the first time Waller's nickname was used on a record label. The second, *Savannah Blues* (Victor 20776), combines very accomplished piano work in the early choruses with some rather less attractive organ playing later on. On both takes, Fats uses an instrumental break to transfer from organ to piano and back again. The first (and originally issued) take is the more balanced performance.

In December 1927, Waller again teamed up with Morris, and produced some of his best-known early band tracks, including *Red Hot Dan* (Victor 21127) and *Geechie* (Victor 21358). Most of these tracks are on *Fats Waller with Morris's Hot Babes* (French RCA 741 062).

A few months later, in March 1928, Fats made the Louisiana Sugar Babes sides, which are extensively discussed in Chapters 2 and 3. The star of these recordings is really Jabbo Smith, whose searing introduction to *Thou Swell* (Victor 21346) and muted solo on *'Sippi* (Victor 21348) rank among his finest work. Other collaborations with James P. Johnson from this period are available on band tracks recorded on June 18, 1928 and November 19, 1929.

The Minor Drag and *Harlem Fuss* are the two band sides to emanate from the session of March 1, 1929 that produced *Handful of Keys*. They are probably the best known of all Waller's pre-Rhythm band sides and have been reissued numerous times.

The March 1, 1929 band adopted the name Fats Waller and his Buddies, and the same name was used on two further sessions later in the year on September 30 and December 18. The personnel on each occasion was different. In March it was the hastily assembled five-piece described by Eddie Condon as having been got together on the strength of last minute telephone calls. That for the September

Albert Nicholas, a member of the large Fats Waller and his Buddies recording group.

session is altogether larger – virtually a big band. Opinion has varied about the personnel, but it now seems to be the consensus that the trumpeter is Henry Allen (taking time off from Luis Russell's orchestra) and at least one of the reeds is Albert Nicholas (also from Russell's band). The propulsive bass playing is that of Al Morgan, and the drumming is by Gene Krupa. There is a rather dire vocal quartet (the Four Wanderers) who contribute to both the tracks recorded on the date. *Lookin' Good But Feelin' Bad* and *I Need Someone Like You* (both Victor V38086) are distinguished by some very fine trombone playing by Jack Teagarden, who, on *Lookin' Good*, catches the Luis Russell mood of his colleagues and turns in a solo very much in the style of J. C. Higginbotham. *Lookin' Good* has the feel of an arranged number, with scored sections for the reeds. *I Need Someone* has a far more impromptu feel about it, and it is evident that what arrangement there is is a fairly hasty one. This time Teagarden turns in a solo that is unmistakably his own in tone, phrasing, and construction.

The December date is also one which draws on the resources of the Russell band. Pops Foster is on bass, and Allen and Nicholas are joined by their other colleagues, Will Johnson (banjo), Charlie Holmes (on alto), and J. C. Higginbotham himself.

Among the December tracks, there are distinct arrangements with synchronized breaks and riffs. On the slowish blues *Ridin' But Walkin'* (Victor V38119) Fats's long trills behind some of the solos detract from the "bluesiness" of the performance, which is otherwise very much in the Russell mode. *Won't You Get Off It, Please?* (also V38119) is worthy of the best of Russell's band in both arrangement and performance, with fine solos from Allen, Larry Binyon (tenor), and Higginbotham. The other two tracks frame some less than wonderful vocals by Orlando Roberson, and *When I'm Alone*, (V38110) takes some time to get going, although it has a fine Waller solo once it does. Both the larger "Buddies" sessions are on the French RCA 741 094.

Although Fats made several more sides with other bandleaders, from Ted Lewis and Jack Teagarden to Eddie Condon and Max Kaminsky, there are two other collaborations to be mentioned here. The first is a set of eight takes of seven tracks in the distinguished company of McKinney's Cotton Pickers (a band which is the subject of John Chilton's fine study *McKinney's Music*), and the second comprises the four titles that Fats cut (in eight takes) with Billy Banks's Rhythmakers.

The French RCA company have again managed to present the

most recent and comprehensive reissue of the McKinney's sessions on *The Complete McKinney's Cotton Pickers Vols. 1–4* (two double albums PM 42407 and 43258), and these contain all the sides that Waller made with the band in an altogether more satisfactory collaboration with Don Redman than the Henderson sides discussed above.

Finally, the Rhythmakers, with Henry Allen, Pee Wee Russell, Jack Bland, Eddie Condon, Pops Foster, and Zutty Singleton, is one of the greatest (and hottest) bands ever to have recorded. The late Philip Larkin described it as a band that "recalls an age when a jazzman was a jazzman and could play pretty well anything with any other jazzmen."[2] Fats's contribution was some swinging piano choruses and much of the drive of the excellent rhythm section. It is a matter of long-term controversy as to whether he is also the falsetto vocalist on *Mean Old Bed Bug Blues* but this author remains unconvinced, preferring to leave the mystery unsolved and revel in the glorious band sound. There are good reissues on CBS and VJM.

THE RHYTHM

The output of this band over its nine-year life is so great as to defy the kind of survey that has been possible for the other areas of Waller's recordings. There are two ways to approach this enormous corpus of material: first to treat each significant change of personnel as a means of dividing the discs into categories, and second to identify broad similarities in the songs that were recorded and the band's treatment of them, cutting across the whole chronological period from 1934 to 1943. Adopting both methods leads us to start with the first group of recordings from 1934.

The sides with Ben Whittet (or Whitted, according to Benny Waters) are an inspiring debut for the band (even if the clarinetist's playing was not up to the standard of his successors), and *A Porter's Love Song* and *Do Me a Favor* (both Victor 24648) are the outstanding tracks from this first session of May 16, 1934. Gene Sedric's arrival for the next session led to some good sides, with Billy Taylor's bass contributing to the general lift of the rhythm section, while the subsequent September 28 date has the rather insipid Mezz Mezzrow on reeds, and the addition (unusually for this band) of Floyd O'Brien on trombone. At least the larger front line allows some full riffs, and these are very effective on the out-chorus of *How Can You Face Me?* (Victor 24737), which also has a fine trombone solo from O'Brien.

The two sessions with Bill Coleman (November 7, 1934 and January 5, 1935) are the high point in the first year of the band's existence. Almost any of the tracks recorded then rank with Waller's finest work, and the presence of the trumpeter at his lyrical best inspires the others in the band to better-than-normal playing.

The choicest sides here are *Believe It Beloved* (Victor 24808), *Dream Man* (Victor 24801) and *Breakin' the Ice* (Victor 24826) from November 7, 1934 and *I'm a Hundred Percent for You* (Victor 24863) and *Night Wind* (Victor 24853) (the latter containing some fine organ work by Fats) from January 5, 1935.

The arrival of Rudy Powell in the group, and the return of Autrey, produced yet another subtle change in the band sound. Autrey's blunter, more forceful trumpet was balanced by the incisive clarinet of Powell, altogether less "classical" in tone than Sedric, and with a vocal edge (produced by humming or singing into the instrument while playing) that is reminiscent of the work of Edmond Hall. The second session by this line-up, from May 1935, produced one of Waller's all-time hits, *I'm Gonna Sit Right Down and Write Myself a Letter* (Victor 25044), as well as the rip-roaring *Lulu's Back in Town* (Victor 25063) (with a fine solo from Powell) and *You're the Cutest One* (Victor 25039). This latter track is redolent of the Mary Lou Williams–Snub Mosley tune *Pretty-eyed Baby*, in terms of both the lyric and parts of the melody. The performance here is a laid back two-beat, Harry Dial's drumming (with its sporadic bass drum accents) recalling his days with Fate Marable on the steamers down to New Orleans.

At this point, in mid-1935, we know that the big band had made its first tours, and the personnel of the Rhythm went through a rather fluid patch. First Dial left, to be replaced not (as he tells us in his autobiography) by Slick Jones, but by Arnold "Scrippy" Boling (or Bolden). Casey's place was taken for some six months by James Smith. Discographers have disagreed about the identity of the clarinetist on the June 24, 1935 date, at first (no doubt on account of the lower register work and a second rather decorative "creole" chorus on *There'll Be Some Changes Made* (Bluebird 10332), and the pretty backing to the great hit *My Very Good Friend the Milkman* (Victor 25075)), ascribing the session to Gene Sedric. However, there is no doubt that the stomping alto solo on the second take of *Sweet Sue* (unissued on 78) is by Rudy Powell, as is the brilliant clarinet work on the riotously swinging *Dinah* (Victor 25471) and the swingingly riotous *Twelfth Street Rag* (Victor 25087). The session as a whole was remarkably productive, both in terms of a major hit, and of substantial jazz content of great quality. In addition to the above tracks several more were cut, including the little known but driving *There's Going to Be the Devil to Pay* (Victor 25078).

The next two sessions were made by the same personnel (Autrey, Powell, Smith, Turner, and Boling), and gems include *Truckin'* (Victor 25116), *Sugar Blues* (Victor 25194), *Rhythm and Romance* (Victor 25131), and *I'm on a See Saw* (Victor 25120).

At the end of November 1935, Sedric returned to the Rhythm, and Yank Porter joined on drums. The band was at a high point and produced the commercial recording of Fats's film success *I've Got My Fingers Crossed* (Victor 25211), as well as a group of other attractive sides, including the hit song *When Somebody Thinks You're Wonderful* (Victor 25222).

The year 1936 was a remarkably consistent one for the band, producing a large volume of recordings. Casey rejoined in April, and there were several changes of drummer, Boling and Porter alternating from one session to another, and Slick Jones making his first appearances on August 1. The finest session was cut on June 8, and consists entirely of instrumentals, including *Black Raspberry Jam/*

THE RECORDS · 157

Paswonky (Victor 25359) and *Fractious Fingering* (Victor 25652). On Christmas Eve the band recorded two of its best ever tracks, with Herman Autrey in inspired form. *Nero* (Victor 25498) has a passage after the vocal where Slick Jones goes into a latin rhythm under sustained growls from Autrey, which they come out of in four–four time, a device which propels the momentum of the piece forward for the trumpeter's solo. But it is *I'm Sorry I Made You Cry* (Victor 25515) on which Autrey really shines, the rhythm section providing him with perfect support as he shrills into his upper register, pausing for effect between his high notes in a manner reminiscent of Armstrong or Hot Lips Page.

All but the West Coast session in 1937 was with the same group as on Christmas Eve 1936 (Autrey, Sedric, Casey, Jones, and Turner). During the year the band's material turned towards the more overtly commercial, the beginning, perhaps, of a record company philosophy that there were some songs that only Fats could do anything with. Amusing ditties like *Spring Cleaning, You're My Dish*, and *She's Tall, She's Tan, She's Terrific* have done little to enhance Waller's reputation with those looking for meaningful jazz quality in his work, and these same critics tend to overlook the fact that 1937 also produced the 12-inch 78 masterpiece of *Blue Turning Grey Over You/Honeysuckle Rose* (Victor 36206). These two extended instrumentals are brilliantly fitted to the slightly longer playing time of the larger record, and are classic performances by a tight-knit, regular working band, with variations in tone color and accompanimental shading, as well as special effects like Slick Jones's eccentric vibes playing. On *Honeysuckle Rose* Fats contributes a memorable left-hand riff behind Sedric, before producing one of his best piano solos in a band context, in which he manages to extend the right-hand motif of the middle eight through into the succeeding four bars, giving the remarkable effect of a solo that appears to break down the 32-bar structure of the piece without actually doing so.

1937 was also the year in which Fats recorded a piece of gentle mayhem which has come to be synonymous with his "good time"

Harlem image: *The Joint Is Jumpin'* (Victor 25689). In the same year, his West Coast Rhythm, with Paul Campbell, Al Morgan, *et al.*, made a set of recordings which include *Every Day's a Holiday* (Victor 25749). In these the tone colors achieved by a band with his conventional instrumentation, but different players, make a good contrast with those produced by his regular line-up.

In early 1938, Cedric Wallace joined the band on bass, and the Rhythm continued to turn out a fairly commercial mixture with some jazz gems buried in most of the sessions. The Continental Rhythm made its recordings in England the same year. These tracks are reissued on EMI's "Retrospect Series" on EG 26 0442 1, but have found their way onto various earlier compilations. The two tracks with organ, *Ain't Misbehavin'* and *Don't Try Your Jive on Me* (HMV BD 5415), are marginally less successful than those on which Fats plays piano, where both rhythm section and front line sound more at ease,

Slick Jones.

although the accomplished young George Chisholm sounds unruffled throughout.

Back in New York, Fats recorded his club and radio theme tunes *Yacht Club Swing* (Bluebird 10035) and *The Spider and the Fly* (Bluebird 10025), the latter typical of a kind of song in which a skillfully crafted arrangement presented a simple vocal with a "shout back" from the rest of the band.

Before Fats returned to England in 1939, the Rhythm took part in two further sessions, on January 19 and March 9. The high spot from the first of these is Herman Autrey's playing on take 2 of *A Good Man Is Hard to Find* (unissued on 78) where he takes a splendid solo over the traditional breaks. The same session produced the jump tune *Hold Tight* (Bluebird 10116) and one of Fats's best sides on Hammond organ with his band, *Kiss Me with Your Eyes* (Bluebird 10136). The March session produced another hit in the form of *Tain't What You Do* (Bluebird 10192).

After Fats's return from Europe, his first American recordings have two new band members, drummer Larry Hinton and the alto saxophonist (erroneously listed as a tenor player in the *Storyville* discography and in Brian Rust's *Jazz Records*) Chauncey Graham. There is a storming alto solo (in a very rhythm-and-blues style) on *What a Pretty Miss* (Bluebird 10437).

In August 1939, Slick Jones was back on drums, but the long-serving Al Casey was replaced by the guitarist John Smith. (Smith was later to take Danny Barker's place with Cab Calloway, and was still playing in the mid-1980s with Panama Francis's Savoy Sultans.) The other change was the arrival of John "Bugs" Hamilton on trumpet. The band made a particularly fine recording of *Squeeze Me* (Bluebird 10405), which makes an interesting contrast (in respect of Fats's piano work) with Willie "the Lion" Smith's solo version recorded (under the title *Boy in a Boat*) for Commodore the same year.

In November 1939, the same line-up recorded Fats's famous hit *Your Feet's Too Big* (Bluebird 10500), as well as the old traditional jazz standard *Darktown Strutters' Ball* (Bluebird 10573). This latter title,

Fats and his Rhythm, 1941.

with its dated and somewhat racist lyric, comes in for a more than usually ironic commentary from the Harmful Little Armful, as he shouts over the first instrumental chorus after his vocal "Ah! Sepia Town . . . Look at my little bronzed body."

The line-up of the band continued the same into 1940, with Al Casey returning on July 16 for a session that produced *Fats Waller's Original E Flat Blues* (Bluebird 10858). This group remained relatively constant as a unit and as the core of the big band into 1941, recording its finest piece of out and out jazz on October 1, 1941 in the form of *Buck Jumpin'* (Bluebird 11324); this is an extended solo for Al Casey, placing him in the very first rank of jazz guitarists. By December 1941, Autrey had returned on trumpet, and the drum chair had been taken over by Arthur Trappier.

The final session by the Rhythm was made in July 1942, in the company of the vocal group the Deep River Boys, and with Hamilton back on trumpet. *Swing Out to Victory* (Bluebird 11569) has some very fine drum breaks by Trappier, and is a jazzy performance; it contrasts with the rather syrupy singing of the Deep River Boys on *By the Light of the Silvery Moon* (also 11569) during which one constantly expects a Spike Jones interruption which never arrives. After this recording date the AFM recording ban came into force, and Waller's last band sides are miscellaneous radio shots and the very fine tracks from the film *Stormy Weather*, discussed in Chapter 4.

If this concludes the personnel-based study, then it is worth drawing attention to one or two related styles of performance which can be seen in the various stages of the Rhythm's output.

First, many of Fats's performances point in the direction of jump or rhythm-and-blues-based music. Songs with shout-back vocals from the band come into this category, notably *Hold Tight* (Bluebird 10116) and *Stop Pretending* (Bluebird 10829). The June 28, 1939 session with Chauncey Graham has a similar jump feel about it.

Second, Fats used light riff-based themes for his broadcasts, and *Yacht Club Swing* (Bluebird 10035), *Swinga-Dilla Street* (Bluebird 10858), and *Panting in the Panther Room* (Bluebird 11175) typify these. Here we can hear Waller on piano or organ backing up tenor riffs with his left hand (or pedalboard) and playing a sparser than usual keyboard role in the manner of Basie. Throughout the recording career of the Rhythm the band was required to make a reasonable quota of instrumental tracks, and it is worth seeking these out since they normally have a fuller jazz content than many of the vocal sides.

Finally, Fats performed a particular style of simple, repetitive popular song in a manner uniquely his own. *Your Feet's Too Big*, or its sequel *Your Socks Don't Match* (Bluebird 30-0814), are good examples. So too are *Shortnin' Bread* (Bluebird 11078) and *The Spider and the Fly* (Bluebird 10205) (the last named is particularly attractive with its simple linking phrase between choruses, and

Sedric's memorable contribution on clarinet). Fats may be criticized in some serious quarters for such light-hearted work, but these tracks contain the essence of his great popular appeal, which came more from simplicity, memorability, and smartly professional arrangements than from the jokiness, shouted comments, and cod vocals which Fats applied to some of the more intractable material he was required to record.

All in all the sheer volume of the Rhythm's output and its remarkable consistency make this body of recorded work a treasure trove of interest for those prepared to take the time to search through it.

THE BIG BAND

In direct contrast to the prolific output of the small band, Fats's orchestra made very few recordings, and its work is confined to four Victor sessions and one airshot.

The first big-band session dates from December 4, 1935, and produced the version of *I Got Rhythm* (HMV HE2902) discussed in Chapter 3. The same band produced two takes of *Fat and Greasy* (unissued on 78), which had a shout-back vocal from the band, and a rather lame arrangement of *Functionizin'* (also HE2902). There is enlivening soprano playing from Emmett Mathews, however, and the cutting contest on *I Got Rhythm* is well worth hearing. A slightly changed version of this band is responsible for some rather muddy airshots from the Rudy Vallee Show, broadcast on June 4, 1936. These (including a big-band version of *I've Got My Fingers Crossed*) have been issued on Ember CJS 839.

By 1938, the swing big bands had grown enormously in popularity, and Fats had considerably overhauled the style of his arrangements to draw them into line with public taste. Among his April 12 big-band recordings were several gems, including a piece that he briefly adopted as a theme tune, *Hold My Hand* (Victor 26045), and *Let's Break the Good News* (Victor 25830). The reed playing is still a bit undisciplined, but there is some particularly fine trumpet work by a team made up from the two principal trumpeters with the Rhythm, Autrey and Hamilton, plus Nathaniel Williams.

Autrey and Hamilton were paired again (this time with Bob Williams on third trumpet) in the 1941 big-band recordings. This July 1 set included only four tunes, among them the popular *Chant of the Groove* (Bluebird 11262) and (on Bluebird 11296) *The Rump Steak Serenade*, which, complete with shout-back, was one of the odes to food and eating which Fats found himself compelled to record from time to time. Here the rhythm playing is more modern in flavor than on the earlier big-band tracks, but the material is not so interesting musically as that of the 1938 records.

Finally, the big band came into the studio in March 1942. Its most interesting side from that date is the *Jitterbug Waltz* (Bluebird 11518) – a catchy tune framed by some attractive Hammond organ playing by Fats. On the recorded evidence alone, Fats's big-band work is insignificant in comparison with that of his six piece band. However, we know that the band worked regularly and traveled for much of Fats's bandleading career. It may well have been a combination of economic advantage and the application of a tried and tested formula that kept the Rhythm recording regularly, while the big band did so infrequently. Whatever else, it is made clear by most people who heard it that the true sound of Fats's big band is not adequately recorded on any of its surviving discs.

That Fats was a capable big-band leader is not in doubt, but ironically it is the December 18, 1929 session with his "Buddies" that gives the most tantalizing hint of how he sounded in the context of a big band. It is interesting to speculate how Fats would have sounded in the late 1930s surrounded (as Armstrong was) by musicians of the caliber of the Luis Russell band. But then, as Fats himself might have said, in a fitting epilog to this survey of his recordings, "One never knows, do one?"

Programme for the 1944 Memorial tribute to Fats at Carnegie Hall.

NOTES

CHAPTER 1

1 "These too have words about Fats," *Coda*, May 1963, p. 25.
2 Author's interview with Stanley Shepherd, October 1986.
3 Fox (1960), p. 77.
4 Smith (1964), pp. 131–2.
5 Brown (1986), p. 167.
6 Barker (1986), p. 140.
7 Willie "The Lion" Smith: "Fats my friend," *Coda*, May 1963, p. 10.
8 *Ibid.*
9 Shapiro and Hentoff (1955), p. 249.
10 Wright (1992), p. 4, has a full list of the eleven children, based on correspondence with Maurice Waller, as follows: Charles A. (b. Sept. 1890; d. in infancy); Edward Lawrence (b. 1892); William Robert (b. 1893); Alfred Winslow (b. 1895; d. 1905); Ruth Adeline (b. 1902; d. 1905); May Naomi (b. 1903); Thomas Wright (b. May 21, 1904); Esther (b. 1906); Samuel (b. 1907); unnamed boy died at birth (b. and d. 1909); Edith Salome (b. July 25, 1910).
11 Al Hoyt: "Mother knew Fats," *Coda*, May 1963, p. 5.
12 Shapiro and Hentoff (1955), p. 249.
13 Eubie Blake: "About Fats," *Coda*, May 1963, p. 10.
14 *Coda*, May 1963, p. 27.
15 *Ibid.*
16 *Ibid.*, p. 29.
17 Darensbourg (1987), p. 122.

18 *Coda*, May 1963, p. 25.

19 Brown (1985), p. 109.

20 Interview with Conover from "It's Off The Record," WABC, New York, September 23, 1943; included on "The Fats Waller Story" (Radiola 2MR 112113).

21 Harrison Smith: "About Fats," *Coda*, May 1963, p. 9.

22 "T. W. (Fats) Waller, pianist, composer: noted negro artist of stage screen and radio dies on train at age of 39," *New York Times*, Thursday, December 16, 1943.

23 Hammond (1977).

24 Don Redman: "A legend in his own time," *Coda*, May 1963, p. 14.

25 Luckey Roberts: "A kind of jazz poet," *Coda*, May 1963, p. 10.

26 The most valiant attempt to list all pieces associated with Waller as composer is Laurie Wright's "Alphabetical listing of known Waller compositions," in Wright (1992), p. 426 ff. This includes several title variations, as well as pieces either not published as being by Waller, but where a copyright application in his name exists, or vice versa. To determine those compositions actually copyrighted in Waller's name, a survey has been published by the English researcher Howard Rye. His "Chronological listing of Fats Waller copyrights" is in Wright (1992), p. 441 ff.

27 The full and extraordinary story of Razaf's background is in Barry Singer: *Black and Blue: The Life and Lyrics of Andy Razaf* (New York, Schirmer, 1992).

28 Andy Razaf: "Fats Waller," *Metronome*, January 1944; reprinted in *Coda*, May 1963, p. 2.

29 Author's interview with Harry Dial, October 24, 1986.

30 Abram Chasins (1957).

31 Nils Hellström: "A clown – but an outstanding pianist," *Orkester Journalen*, October 1938, translated by Alf Lavér and reprinted in Wright (1992), pp. 183–4.

CHAPTER 2

1 Laurie Wright speculates that Waller joined the revue as early as December 9, 1922, for a run at the Lincoln Theater in New York. The first reference to the act as it was to be described by Garvin Bushell is in the *New York Age*, May 5, 1923, which details an

appearance by "Liza and 'Shuffle Along' Six" at Fitchburg, Mass. For more details see Wright (1992), p. 17.

2 Nat Hentoff: "Garvin Bushell and New York jazz in the 1920s," *The Jazz Review*, April 1959, p. 16 (the third of three articles).

3 Garvin Bushell interviewed by Mark Tucker, Las Vegas, Nevada, July 10, 1986.

4 *Ibid.*

5 Basie (1986), pp. 55 ff.

6 Waller (1977), pp. 55 ff. In this, Maurice suggests that the Kentucky Club booking was in 1924, but as Laurie Wright points out (Wright (1992), p. 22), the Kentucky did not open until 1925, and there is a review of Ellington and Waller in *Billboard*, December 5, 1925, that firmly places this appearance in that year.

7 Barker (1986), p. 141.

8 *New York Age*, January 22, 1927; *New York Amsterdam News*, January 19, 1927.

9 It seems as if Waller originally planned to appear at the Metropolitan Theater in Chicago, as *Variety* of March 2 announced that he would move there from New York's Lincoln, but he was certainly at the Vendome by March 19 when Dave Peyton referred to it in his "Musical Bunch" column in the *Chicago Defender*.

10 Collier (1983), p. 156.

11 *Chicago Defender*, March 26, 1927.

12 *Chicago Defender*, April 30, 1927.

13 Dance (1977), p. 35.

14 Harrison Smith: "About Fats," *Coda*, May 1963, p. 9.

15 *Variety*, March 7, 1928.

16 Bordman (1978), p. 437.

17 Reviews all quoted in Bordman (1978).

18 Andy Razaf: "Fats Waller," *Metronome*, January 1944; reprinted in *Coda*, May 1963, p. 2.

19 Garvin Bushell interviewed by Mark Tucker, Las Vegas, Nevada, July 10, 1986.

20 Author's interview with Jabbo Smith, October 1986.

21 Brown (1986), pp. 202–3.

22 Wright (1992) confirms the dates of Waller's incarceration and eventual release; and T. Magnusson: "Fats Waller with Gene

Austin on the Record," *Journal of Jazz Studies*, Vol. 4, No. 1 (1976), p. 75, dissects the evidence for Austin's involvement (or not) in bailing Fats out in October 1928.

23 The only copyright record of a Waller composition to mention *Load of Coal* was filed by Santly Brothers in November 1929 for *Honeysuckle Rose*, which the same publisher had actually filed without explicit connection to a show two months earlier, in September. This may mean that *Load of Coal* was a short-lived revue that ran briefly after *Hot Chocolates* had opened, and which was therefore not only wrongly placed in the chronological sequence, but also given exaggerated importance in Kirkeby's biography of Waller. Razaf, however, mentions it as a production that they were "working on for Connie," and confirms that *Honeysuckle Rose* was part of that production. I have therefore retained the originally published chronology in my text, based on Razaf's reminiscences, in Andy Razaf: "Fats Waller," *Metronome*, January 1944; reprinted in *Coda*, May 1963, p. 2.

24 Wells (1971), pp. 26–7.

25 Waters (1985), p. 34.

26 *Ibid.*

27 Wells (1971), pp. 26–7.

28 *Melody Maker*, April 10, 1954.

29 Milton "Mezz" Mezzrow: "Fats Waller," *Bulletin du Hot Club de France*, May 1952, No. 18, p. 3, translated by the author.

30 Andy Razaf: "Fats Waller," *Metronome*, January 1944; reprinted in *Coda*, May 1963, p. 2.

31 *New York Times*, June 21, 1929.

32 Milton "Mezz" Mezzrow: "Fats Waller," *Bulletin du Hot Club de France*, May 1952, No. 18, p. 3, translated by the author.

33 Howard Rye's researches into Waller's copyrights, published in Wright (1992), suggest that there was a much more gradual transfer of the rights in Fats's composition to Mills Music than the single reported transfer of several songs on July 17, and that some were registered by Mills in late June and early July, suggesting that the $500 was most likely a stage payment. Wright also reports that Waller was employed by publisher Joe Davis for part of the time he was writing *Hot Chocolates*. This also suggests that Waller would be less likely to sell a sequence of copyrights for an outright fee.

The results of his labors with Davis were copyrighted and (mostly) published later in 1929.

34 *Chicago Defender*, February 22, 1930.
35 *Chicago Defender*, August 16, 1930.
36 Kirkeby (1966), p. 220.
37 Joey Nash: "Memories of Fats Waller," *Jazz*, January 1966, p. 12 ff.
38 Michael Hanlon: "Talking with jazzman Herman Autrey," *Toronto Globe and Mail*, February 12, 1965.
39 Barker (1986), p. 166.
40 Brown (1986), p. 54.

CHAPTER 3

1 Kirkeby (1966), p. 151.
2 Lester "Spare Rib" Nichols: "Hollering over the ensemble," *Coda*, May 1963, p. 25.
3 Machlin (1985).
4 Barker (1986), p. 147.
5 Letter to the author from Art Rollini, October 15, 1986.
6 Author's interview with Harry Dial, October 24, 1986.
7 Hugues Panassié: "Herman Autrey," *Jazz Journal*, December 1955; George W. Kay: "Herman Autrey recalls the early days," *Jazz Journal*, October 1969, p. 10.
8 Author's interview with Al Casey, November 23, 1998.
9 Author's interview with Harry Dial, October 24, 1986.
10 Coleman (1981), translated by the author. (NB: At the time of the first edition of this book, the English translation of Coleman's memoirs had yet to be published by Macmillan and the only available version was in French.)
11 Madeleine Gautier: "Sedric vous parle de Fats Waller," *Bulletin du Hot Club de France*, No. 28 (May 1953), p. 3, translated by the author.
12 Author's interview with Harry Dial, October 24, 1986; George W. Kay: "Herman Autrey recalls the early days," *Jazz Journal*, October 1969, p. 10.
13 Coleman (1981), translated by the author.
14 Author's interview with Harry Dial, October 24, 1986.

15 Hugues Panassié: Fats Waller Vol. 4 (French RCA 430 209) (liner note), translated by the author.
16 Author's interview with Harry Dial, October 24, 1986.
17 *Ibid.*
18 *Ibid.*
19 Both Thomas and Flemming are quoted in *Coda*, May 1963.
20 Michael Hanlon: "Talking with jazzman Herman Autrey," *Toronto Globe and Mail*, February 12, 1965.
21 Author's interview with Harry Dial, October 24, 1986.
22 John McLellan: "The jazz scene: Fats Waller stirs interest," *Boston Traveler*, December 3, 1957.

CHAPTER 4

1 Clayton (1986), p. 47.
2 Slim Thompson: "Fats Waller," *Coda*, May 1963, p. 19.
3 According to Wright (1992), p. 106, Waller also recorded *Oh, Susanna!*, which was not used in the film, and he can be heard on the soundtrack, playing piano on a version of *I'm Shootin' High*.
4 I was unable to find a corroborating press cutting concerning Waller's appearance in Philadelphia, and it may be that I was looking for evidence from the wrong city, since Laurie Wright subsequently found that the band appeared in Pittsburgh on June 28, 1935, while the film was being screened there (Wright (1992), p. 104).
5 Nat Hentoff: "Morgan: riverboat bass," *The Jazz Record*, February 1946, pp. 11–13.
6 Val Wilmer: "The Lee Young story," *Jazz Journal*, Vol. 24, No. 1 (January 1961), p. 3.
7 David Meeker (1977).
8 Dave Dixon: "The Jugglin' jive of Fats Waller," *Fats Waller Live, Vol. 3* (GOJ 1041) (liner note), 1986.
9 *Ibid.*
10 Karl Gurt zur Heide: "Eugene Porter," *Footnote*, Vol. 7, No. 6 (August/September 1976), p. 17.

CHAPTER 5

1 Hugues Panassié (1946). Hammond's *Melody Maker* article

concerning the "consular difficulty" about Waller's possible visit to England appeared in October 1932.

2 *The Stage*, July 18, 1938.
3 *The Stage*, August 11, 1938.
4 *Melody Maker*, August 13, 1938.
5 *The Stage*, August 18, 1938.
6 *The Stage*, August 25, 1938.
7 Iain Lang: "A pilgrim's progress," in Ken Williamson (1960), p. 123 ff.
8 George Chisholm: "Jammin' in England," *Coda*, May 1963, p. 16.
9 Jeffrey P. Green: "Bix in Barbados: Dave Wilkins, trumpet," *Storyville*, No. 118 (April–May 1985), p. 146.
10 Iain Lang: "A pilgrim's progress," in Ken Williamson (1960).
11 Howard Rye: "Fats Waller in Britain"; Howard Rye and Josephine Beaton: "Fats Waller's British diary," *Storyville*, No. 81 (February–March 1979), p. 83 and pp. 86 ff.
12 Jeff Atterton: "There'll never be another Fats," *Coda*, May 1963, p. 16.
13 Brown (1985), p. 99.

CHAPTER 6

1 "A note from Fats," in Wright (1992), p. 1.
2 Wright (1992), p. 221.
3 Wright (1992), p. 237.
4 Author's interview with Franz Jackson, July 1998.
5 Kirkeby (1966), p. 229.
6 *Ibid*.
7 Dick Wellstood: "Waller to Wellstood to Williams to chaos," *The Jazz Review*, August 1960, p. 10.

CHAPTER 7

1 Hugues Panassié: *Fats Waller Vol. 4* (French RCA 430 209) (liner note), translated by the author.
2 Larkin (1970).

BIBLIOGRAPHY

The following books were used in preparing the text.

Barker, Danny: *A Life in Jazz* (edited by Alyn Shipton) (London, Macmillan, 1986).

Basie, Count: *Good Morning Blues* (as told to Albert Murray) (London, Heinemann, 1986).

Bernhardt, Clyde E. B.: *I Remember* (edited by Sheldon Harris) (Philadelphia, University of Pennsylvania Press, 1986).

Bordman, Gerald M.: *The American Musical Theatre* (New York, Oxford University Press, 1978).

Boulton, David: *Jazz in Britain* (London, W. H. Allen, 1958).

Brown, Ron: *Georgia on My Mind: The Nat Gonella Story* (Portsmouth, Milestone, 1985).

Brown, Scott E.: *James P. Johnson: A Case of Mistaken Identity* (includes discography by Robert Hilbert) (Metuchen, NJ, Scarecrow, 1986).

Charters, Samuel B. and Kunstadt, L.: *Jazz: A History of the New York Scene* (2nd edition) (New York, Da Capo, 1981).

Chasins, Abram: *Speaking of Pianists* (New York, Knopf, 1957).

Chilton, John: *Who's Who of Jazz* (4th edition) (London, Macmillan, 1985).

Clayton, Buck: *Buck Clayton's Jazz World* (assisted by Nancy Miller Elliott) (London, Macmillan, 1986).

Coleman, Bill: *Trumpet Story* (Paris, Editions Cana, 1981).

Collier, James Lincoln: *Louis Armstrong* (New York, Oxford University Press, 1983).

Dance, Stanley: *The World of Earl Hines* (New York, Scribner, 1977).

Darensbourg, Joe: *Telling It Like It Is* (edited by Peter Vacher) (London, Macmillan, 1987); published in the USA as *Jazz Odyssey* (Baton Rouge, Louisiana State University Press, 1987).

Dial, Harry: *All This Jazz about Jazz* (Chigwell, Essex, Storyville, 1984).

Fox, Charles: *Fats Waller* (London, Cassell, 1960).

Fox, Ted: *Showtime at the Apollo* (New York, Holt, Rinehart, and Winston, 1983).

Hadlock, Richard: *Jazz Masters of the Twenties* (New York, Macmillan, 1965).

Hammond, John: *John Hammond on the Record* (Harmondsworth, Penguin, 1977).

Harrison, Max: *A Jazz Retrospect* (Newton Abbot, David and Charles, 1976).

Jones, Max: *Talking Jazz* (London, Macmillan, 1987).

Kirkeby, Ed (with Schiedt, Duncan P. and Traill, Sinclair: *Ain't Misbehavin'* (includes *The Music of Thomas "Fats" Waller*, a discography compiled by the "Storyville Team") (New York, Dodd Mead, 1966).

Lang, Iain: "A Pilgrim's Progress," in *This Is Jazz* (edited by Ken Williamson) (London, Newnes, 1960).

Larkin, Philip: *All What Jazz* (London, Faber, 1970).

Machlin, Paul S.: *Stride: The Music of Fats Waller* (Boston, Twayne, 1985).

Meeker, David: *Jazz in the Movies* (London, Talisman, 1977).

Nash, Jay Robert and Ross, Stanley Ralph: *The Motion Picture Guide* (Vols. I–XII) (Chicago, Cinebooks, 1987).

Panassié, Hugues: *Douze Années de jazz* (Paris, Correa, 1946).

Rust, Brian: *Jazz Records 1897–1942* (Chigwell, Essex, Storyville, 1982).

Shapiro, Nat and Hentoff, Nat (eds): *Hear Me Talkin' to Ya* (London, Peter Davies, 1955).

Smith, Willie "the Lion": *Music on My Mind* (edited by George Hoefer) (New York, Doubleday, 1964).

Vance, Joel: *Fats Waller: His Life and Times* (Chicago, Contemporary Books, 1977).

Waller, Maurice and Calabrese, Anthony: *Fats Waller* (New York, Schirmer, 1977).

Waters, Benny: *The Key to a Jazzy Life* (Toulouse, France, Les Arts Graphiques, 1985).

Wells, Dicky: *The Night People* (as told to Stanley Dance) (Boston, Crescendo, 1971).

Wright, Laurie: *Fats in Fact* (Chigwell, Essex, Storyville, 1992).

INDEX

Printed in Great Britain
by Amazon.co.uk, Ltd.,
Marston Gate.